THE
REDEMPTION OF AFRICA
AND BLACK RELIGION

THE REDEMPTION

OF AFRICA

AND BLACK RELIGION

By St. Clair Drake

wTp

THIRD WORLD PRESS

Chicago, Illinois

INSTITUTE OF THE BLACK WORLD

Atlanta, Georgia

First Edition

Fifth Printing 1991

LCN: 70-171226
ISBN: 0-88378-017-8

Manufactured in the United States of America

Introduction

The richness and complexities which characterize so much of St. Clair Drake's work are fully evident in this Black Paper. For instance, while the essay produced here is currently identified as "Chapter XIX" in the first draft of a major work on the Black Diaspora, and is entitled, "The Redemption of Africa and Black Religion," it is obvious that we are really presented with three important, related thematic lines. The first sketches an overview of the development of African cultures in the New World. From that point of departure, Drake goes on to deal with the experience of black religion in North America and the Caribbean, indicating the crucial role of religion in our struggles towards freedom, identity, and self-determination. Finally, in one of the most original sections of the work, Drake deals with the development of a mode of thinking which he calls, "Ethiopianism," and the concept of "Providential Design" as developed in the centuries of our exile and returns.

Ranging from Africa along the triangular pathways of our sorrows and renewals, disregarding the walls of academic disciplines, Brother Drake establishes connections among our experiences which are crucial for our own inner clarity as African peoples. Many of these black connections of places are, of course, best viewed in Drake's own life.

St. Clair Drake was born in Suffolk, Virginia, and spent his early years there, as well as in Staunton, Virginia, and Pittsburgh, Pennsylvania. At the age of twelve he traveled to Barbados, the birthplace of his father, where he lived with his father's family for over a year, and where the Afro-West Indian way of life made an impression on him which he did not forget. At the age of fourteen, Drake returned to Staunton, Virginia, to live with his mother's people, since at this time his father became International Organizer of the worldwide Universal Negro Improvement Association of Marcus Garvey. During the 1926 convention of the UNIA, his

5

father presented proposals for the establishment of Liberty University (the School of African Philosophy) near Jamestown, Virginia, an institution of which he subsequently became the head, and which attempted to train a successor generation of black leaders for the African struggle.

While attending Hampton Institute, in Virginia, Drake became a close friend of Mbiyu Koinange, the present minister of external affairs of Kenya, and the author of the important book, *The People of Kenya Speak for Themselves* (1954), the most significant African defense of the Kenyan people to emerge during the Mau Mau resistance struggle. It was Koinange who inspired Drake to devote himself to African liberation.

Drake later on, in 1947, came into contact in Britain with the post-Garvey phase of the Pan-African struggle through his friendship with the West Indians, George Padmore, Dr. Peter Milliard, and T. Ras Makonnen, and the future African leader, Kwame Nkrumah, who together in 1944, had merged their efforts into establishing the Pan-African Federation in Manchester, England. This was the organization which spearheaded the holding of the famous Fifth Pan-African Congress (in October, 1945, in Manchester), the first to be held since 1926, and the beacon which signalled to African peoples throughout the world that a new stage of struggle was commencing. The medium through which Drake's interests were fed into the Manchester grouping was the black community of merchant seamen and workers that he had been studying for his doctoral dissertation, in Tiger Bay, the port section of Cardiff, Wales. His thesis was titled, "Value Systems, Social Structure, and Race Relations in the British Isles." Drake found that this community had much wider ties than expected, which would have to be traced. Thence the black workers of Tiger Bay put him in touch with their London circles, and it was there that he was introduced to the great standard-bearer of African political struggle of the inter-war years, George Padmore. The friendship that grew out of this initial contact between St. Clair Drake and George Padmore became increasingly strong with the passage of time and continued on an intimate basis right up until Padmore's death in September, 1959.

Indeed, Drake's introduction to the succeeding phase of the African struggle came through his close ties with Padmore, and

6

led him to six months of teaching in Liberia, in 1954, followed by nine months in the Gold Coast and Nigeria. He returned to Ghana in 1958, and served as head of the department of sociology at the University there until the spring of 1961.

This was a crucial period in African history. Padmore had been brought to Ghana as advisor to President Nkrumah on African Affairs, shortly after independence in 1957, in which position he was to pour all his immense political experience and bring to bear his remarkable organizing genius in the planning and execution of the First Conference of Independent African States and the All-Africa Peoples' Conference, held respectively in April and December, 1958. Drake participated in the latter conference, occupying quite literally a ringside seat, and going so far as to assist Padmore in the planning of the conference and the drafting of some of the important conference resolutions.

The cultural side of the Pan-African struggle, however, has seen St. Clair Drake as much involved as he has been on the political side. The papers he presented at the First and Second Conferences of Black Writers, sponsored by the Society of African Culture in Paris, 1956, and Rome, 1959, were a significant contribution culturally. His assessment of the conferences, as well as a general interpretation of the *negritude* movement, appeared in the article, "Hide My Face? An Essay on Pan-Africanism and Negritude" (*Soon One Morning*, edited by Herbert Hill, 1963). When in 1966 Drake went off to Dakar, Senegal, to attend the First World Festival of Negro Arts, called by President Leopold Senghor to celebrate the full flowering of *negritude* and its achievements, he achieved the singular distinction of being actively present at all the major postwar Pan-African gatherings.

Here in America, Drake has also been associated with the attempts by various organizations to bring Black America into closer identification with the new African presence in world affairs. He was one of the original founding members of the American Society of African Culture (AMSAC) and, later, the American Negro Leadership Conference on Africa.

Throughout this extensive period of close observance of the African liberation struggles, he not only took the time to secure a Doctor's degree in social anthropology with emphasis upon African studies, but he has been able also to assist a new generation of students in gaining a full appreciation of its heritage, as a professor at the University of Liberia, the University of Ghana, and in particular at Roosevelt University in Chicago. He is currently serving as head of the Black Studies program at Stanford University.

Out of this long and close involvement with the various historical strands of the Pan-African movement, on one hand, and close to thirty years of uninterrupted teaching, publishing, and research in the area of African and Afro-American culture, on the other, now emerges St. Clair Drake's long-awaited study, *The Black Diaspora,* of which this BLACK PAPER is the first chapter to be published.

The Institute of the Black World considers it most appropriate to have the work of such a crucial older brother in the struggle as the first product of our new venture in cooperative publishing with Third World Press. In this way we continue to seek to be attuned to the thoughts of the fathers while building new institutions towards the survival and prevailing of our children.

The Redemption
of Africa and Black Religion

Ethiopia, thou land of our fathers,
Thou land where the gods used to be;
As storm clouds at night suddenly gather,

*   *   *

Advance, advance, to victory,
Let Africa be free.
—Anthem of the *Universal Negro*
Improvement Association (1920)

In the city of Addis Ababa, on the highlands of East Africa, there lives a King-Emperor who claims a distinguished royal lineage: Haile Selassie, King of Kings, Elect of God, Conquering Lion of Judah, and Heir to the Throne of Solomon and the Queen of Sheba. Close by his palace is the spot where all of the independent African states have placed the headquarters of their Organization of African Unity (OAU). Almost seventy years before these nations did so, in 1896, the warriors of an indubitably black ruler, among people the anthropologists insist upon calling "Hamites" instead of Negroes, shattered an Italian invading army in these mountains and sent waves of pride coursing throughout the black world. Here, Mussolini returned in 1935, seeking revenge and arousing black anger and gestures of solidarity wherever Negroes lived. Haile Selassie, though not visibly Negro as his distinguished predecessor, became a symbol of courage in the face of betrayal by white men who controlled the League of Nations.

But Ethiopia was a symbol of Black Power long before Menelik II vindicated The Race by defeating a white nation on the battlefield, thus saving his country from conquest by Europeans. During the Middle Ages, it was such a symbol to the Portuguese, Spaniards

9

and Italians who believed that a Christian king named Prester John lived there, who, if found, could aid them in their struggle against the Muslims. Of this the slaves in the New World had no knowledge, but as soon as any among them could read, they discovered the name of Ethiopia in their Bibles and what was said about that ancient kingdom and its peoples inspired them and raised their hopes. Later, when black men from The Diaspora made their first Return, a monthly journal was founded in Freetown, Sierra Leone called *Ethiopia,* and when the *Africa and Sierra Leone Weekly Advertiser* was established in 1885, the editor put the Biblical prophecy at its masthead, "Princes shall come out of Egypt and Ethiopia shall soon stretch forth her hand unto God."

The name of Ethiopia still has the power to move black men. Thousands of Ras Tafarians in the slums of Jamaica have separated themselves from among their fellows and dream of the day when *their* God-King, *Ras Tafari,*[1] Haile Selassie, will send his ships to take them "home." And even among the sophisticates of the black ghettos in the United States, a visit to America by the King of Kings is headline news in the Negro press and the crowds turn out to see him when he pays a visit to Harlem or the South Side of Chicago. And in those crowds are members of a tiny but persistent cult, the *Ethiopian World Federation,* who have a special reason for paying him homage, for he has given them land for a farm and a school in the country that they, alienated from America, call *their* nation.

The people of the Black Diaspora, uprooted and thrown into the New World cauldron and melting pot, have had to grapple for centuries with the problem of how to preserve their dignity and self-esteem in situations where white men held them in slavery, and, then, when emancipation came, refused to accord them the full status of free men and women. The more reflective among them have also been obsessed with the question of "Who are we?" and "Why have we suffered this fate?"—the twin problem of uncertain identity and powerlessness. They knew they were Africans and "of African descent," but white men invested the name of Africa with attributes that brought on feelings of shame. Compen-

---

[1] Ras Tafari was the name of the emperor, Haile Selassie, before he was enthroned.

satory beliefs backed up by convincing authority—great *myths,* the source of every people's deepest strengths—were needed to bolster their self-esteem.

Black people under slavery turned to the Bible to "prove" that a black people, Ethiopians, were powerful and respected when white men in Europe were barbarians; Ethiopia came to symbolize all of Africa; and, throughout the 19th century, the "redemption of Africa" became one important focus of meaningful activity for leaders among New World Negroes. "Ethiopianism" became an energizing myth in both the New World and in Africa itself for those pre-political movements that arose while the powerless were gathering their strength for realistic and rewarding political activity. Its force is now almost spent, but "Ethiopianism" left an enduring legacy to the people who fight for Black Power in the Twentieth Century, and some of its development needs to be understood.

Afro-American
and African-American Cultures

Once the degrading experience of the Middle Passage was over and the indignity of being sold like an animal in the slave mart was behind him, each newly imported African became a member of some New World social system on a plantation, in a mining camp, or in a town. Each individual had been torn out of a familiar cultural setting in which his obligations to his fellowmen and his reciprocal rights and privileges were well defined, even if he happenened to be a slave. In Africa, he was bound by ties of affection and reciprocity to kinsmen and friends, and, even if a slave, was adopted into a kin group where time softened, and sometimes totally wiped out, the invidious distinction. He was not a "chattel." The rules of the game were set by tradition and everyone knew what the characteristics of a "virtuous" man or woman were, whatever the station in life in African society. The mold was shattered as soon as he became one of that nameless mass of individuals designated for the Middle Passage. There was no need in Africa, even under the mild forms of slavery to which a few people were subjected, for them to sing in lamentation. But it is no mystery why, out of the traumatic experience of the trans-Atlantic slave trade and subsequent enslavement, American Negroes came to sing:

> "Sometimes I feel like a motherless child;
> Sometimes I feel like a motherless child—
> A l-o-n-g w-a-y-y-y from home.

When the fact has been accepted that African slaves were men and women like all other human beings, it is not difficult to imagine the depth of their fears, the agony of their anxieties, and the profundity of their griefs and sorrows when they were forcibly expatriated. We are fortunate in having a few personal accounts to

12

confirm our empathy, written by some exceptional human beings who survived the experience, rose above it and left the legacy of their words.

No one can question the fact that some Africans—and perhaps most—resented being torn out of the familiar matrix of existence for a voyage across the sea to live an alien mode of life. The mutinies and suicides aboard ship and the refusals to take food; the cases of "tongue-swallowing" and suicide on the plantations; the sullen demeanor of many slaves on the auction block; the flight of some to the backlands and mountains to become Maroons; the high incidence of "salt water Negroes" among the leaders of revolts—all of this gives convincing testimony that the initial reaction to enslavement was one of intense hostility and sometimes of extreme personal disorganization. What happened immediately after being purchased and handed over to a "master," however, depended upon the social situation in which the individual found himself and of these there was a great variety. The extremes in North America might be illustrated by the difference between the fate of the Senegalese slave girl bought by a couple in Boston who became the first American Negro poetess, Phyllis Wheatley, and some nameless black girl bought by a Southern planter to be taken to his plantations to sate the passions of himself and his cronies. In the West Indies the extremes may be measured by the fate of a house servant on the estate of a resident planter in Barbados as contrasted with that of a cane-cutter in Jamaica on a plantation owned by an absentee landlord and managed by a ruthless drunken "attorney."

Out of the ranks of the favored few came the spies and the informers, but out of this stratum, too, also came creative individuals like the Haitian leader, Toussaint L'Ouverture. The great mass of the slaves had to construct for themselves a society that could put some meaning into their existence other than that of being producers of commodities and of a new generation of slaves for their masters. No longer bound together as family and village units growing food for themselves, they were alienated from the productive process. Land and the cultivation of it could no longer be the critical focus of their interest and emotions as in Africa. The men of honor and prestige, similar to them in color and culture—their elders and chiefs—were now replaced by white men with different values and standards—masters and overseers—with black subalterns

13

to carry out their will toward other black men. Most of the exiled Africans were destined to live out their lives as participants in a new type of society—a plantation system—where one man, an owner or estate manager, had absolute control over every aspect of their lives, could sell them as individuals instead of family groups, and could even take their lives for disobedience if he wished to do so. For slaves who chose compliance rather than defiance—and these understandably were in the majority—the rational reaction was to do the job assigned (though not necessarily well) in return for food and shelter, and to avoid punishment, as well as to size up the situation to see what scanty special awards were available to those who played the game astutely, and to count the costs to be payed for bucking the system. In Africa, such calculations of one's personal welfare were always made with reference to the effect upon kinsmen and in consultation with them. For newly landed slaves these bonds had been ripped asunder. It was each for himself. The cultures of Africa provided no cues for coping with slave-traders and newly acquired "masters."

Men, however, cannot live as completely atomized individuals. Where individuals from the same tribe were placed together in New World work situations, the "tribe," the ethnic group, provided one natural primordial base for binding men together—even though they were not kinsmen. Ethnic solidarity and a sense of ethnic identity persisted wherever it was not deliberately disrupted by the masters or was made impossible by the accident of extreme heterogeneity within a given group of slaves. But, from the beginning, a new bond of solidarity is also apparent on the plantations, a supratribal bond, the tie between "shipmates," the solidarity of those who defined themselves as "We who went through the ordeal of the Middle Passage together." Dyadic relations were quickly established, too, between individuals of the same sex who became friends, and between men and women who pleased each other (though there were seldom enough women to allow all men to find a mate during the first generation), or when new increments of slaves were thrown into a plantation society. Out of the relations between mothers and the children born to them matrifocal family clusters took root, but where possible men and women formed the types of household units in which they had been reared in Africa.

On every plantation a "Creole" culture emerged—a blending of African and European cultural elements with modifications and reinterpretations of material from both sources. Once such a local culture had come into being, any new Africans who were imported were inducted into that culture and did not face the same difficult adjustments as the original group. The extent to which they modified the Creole culture depended upon the size of the new group introduced as well as upon the type of African culture they brought, the roles they were assigned by the master, and the types of personalities among them. In Haiti and Jamaica there was a clear tendency for elements from a variety of African cultures to fuse and form a sub-culture with a system of religion and magic that drew heavily from Dahomey in the case of Haiti, and from the Akan-speaking peoples of the Gold Coast in the case of Jamaica. The configurations were less highly integrated in other Caribbean areas but African "cultural survivals" everywhere provided fixed points of reference for social relations and for philosophical and theological orientation. Occasionally, a common plantation culture welded the slaves together for united action, but always, for the ordinary individual, it provided a scheme of living that put order and meaning into life, allowed people to maintain a sense of worth despite their subordination, and guaranteed them a measure of "enjoyment" if not contentment.

But all individuals in the plantation subculture were not "ordinary" individuals. Some social scientists—notably Elkins, in his book, *Slavery*—have attempted to prove that slavery generated a personality type in the American South, childlike, obsequious, compliant and "devious"—the "Sambo" type and that most of the slaves were "Sambos." Orlando Patterson feels that an equivalent type can be defined for Jamaica, the "Quarshie." (The actual statistical incidence of the type has not been ascertained.) Both point out, however, that under Portuguese and Spanish slave systems this type was probably not in the majority. But whatever type formed the majority in a plantation population, there is abundant evidence to indicate that there were always other social types present, too, artisans who were assigned responsibility and elicited respect from both masters and slaves; those endowed with great intelligence and wisdom to whom lesser men turned for counsel and advice; "bad niggers" as well as "Uncle Toms." Such people expressed,

15

in their total personality, wishes and moods not obvious on the surface that existed as minor aspects of every slave's personality. Their presence on the plantation made them agents of social change.

Of all the social types produced in these New World social systems none were more crucial in the process of social change than the house servants. Exposed to a way of life totally different from that of the slave quarters, thrown into a nexus of interpersonal relations that involved intimacy and affection, they developed as a group apart, marginal and ambivalent in their attitudes toward their cruder fellows and jealously guarding their own privileges. Out of the relations between masters and black women in this stratum, groups of mulattoes came into being who prized their lighter skin color as the symbol of their higher status. On some plantations, mulattoes born from white men's matings with black women of the field did not achieve a privileged status, but exerted an unsettling influence due to their marginal position. In the French West Indies, a "free colored" group formed a distinct social stratum with well-defined privileges not accorded to the blacks. All house servants and free colored persons were bound to the white segment of plantation society by similarity of culture and outlook, and sometimes by kinship. They were both admired and hated by "field Negroes," and were, themselves, often divided in mind and spirit by conflicting loyalties.

But, whatever the fate of an African was to be after he had become a part of plantation society, in the initial stages of enslavement all shared a common experience. At home in Africa, Kofi not only had a name that was of symbolic significane to him, but also had an unambiguous group identity, and was respected as an individual. To make a slave of Kofi he had first to be transformed from a tribesman into a "worthless nigger," a "heathen black." The slave factories and the baracoons on the coast of Africa and the indignities of the Middle Passage were calculated to begin the process. Then the "black" had to be reduced almost to the level of an animal —eyed and poked and felt and bid for in the New World slave marts. The aim was not really to *dehumanize* him, however, but only to *degrade* him, to change him from one kind of human being into another, from an autonomous individual rooted in a culture into a tractable, pliant, human being always responsive to the command of a master or a mistress. The processes of capture and sale were what anthropologists call *rites of separation*, the first stages in an initiation process. There were acts designed to "kill" the old man, a death preparatory to rebirth.

The "seasoning" process was the first step in a *rite of transistion*, in the making of a new man out of Kofi, often a man with a new scoffing name like Caesar, Prince or Pompey, a name without the rich and sometimes mystical meaning of the African name. Planters as well as visitors to plantations have left us numerous accounts of the "breaking-in" or "seasoning" process, but we have a few accounts of it by ex-slaves who were subject to it or witnessed it. The slaves already there, after the plantation had been organized, the bearers of the Creole culture, were allotted a role in the seasoning process. This was never precisely what the masters intended it to be, however, for while the members of the plantation community taught the newcomer how to be a good slave, how to fit in, they also taught him how to maintain his humanity if not always his dignity, and the tricks of survival and of working against the system by subtle sabotage and malingering, about which a great deal of evidence has been compiled.

Occasionally, too, the confrontation between Creoles and "salt water Negroes" became a dialogue about how men should react to enslavement, for, in some cases, the baracoons and the Middle Passage and the auction block had not been traumatic and psychologically devastating enough to break Kofi, to make him accept the status of "worthless nigger" or chattel. Thus, the smooth working of the "seasoning" process was sometimes disturbed by the flight of Creoles to the hills and backlands under Kofi's leadership or participation in rebellions led by him. All of this created folk heroes whose names and exploits were handed down from one generation of plantation dwellers to another and these spread throughout the New World as slaves were sold from plantation to plantation, Caribbean island to Caribbean island, and from the West Indies into North America. In addition to Ananse the Spider, Brer Rabbit and those other clever animals who outwitted the strong ones, the names of clever *people* became a part of the black subculture of the New World. We can be sure that even some Samboes and Quarshies had a sneaking admiration for them. Thus, while the folk culture operated to stabilize the plantation system it also carried within itself elements to reinforce group rebellion in times of crisis.

In addition to a common *African-American* culture that took form in the Caribbean and South America among the mass of the slaves, and an *Afro-American* culture in North America, where pressures for Europeanization were stronger, a sense of *black consciousness* emerged throughout the world of the Diaspora. In Africa, men continued to think of themselves primarily as members of specific tribes. Here and there in the New World, ethnic identification remained, but over-arching and over-riding the tribal focus of identity was an imposed identity. White men defined all Africans as "blacks," *"les noirs."* They might try to divide and rule by favoring one tribe against another on a specific plantation; they might have their stereotypes about which tribes were brave or pusillanimous or produced exciting and seductive women, but in their buying and their selling of men, their suppression of rebellion, and their verbalizations when expressing anger, all were simply "blacks." The slaves' counter-image of themselves was that they were *Africans.* The people of the Diaspora eventually defined Africa as their "home," not some specific local spot from which they came or where their tribe or that of their ancestors lived, but *Africa.* The word, Guinea, in some places, came to symbolize the continent. When a man died his spirit went "home"—to "Guinea" or to *Africa*—the land of black men.

It was inevitable that, given the shifting of slaves from island to island throughout the Caribbean and from the Caribbean to North America, and *vice versa,* an awareness of their wide distribution in the Diaspora would emerge, and that as leaders mobilized *black consciousness* in a bid for Black Power in local situations through risings and the formation of Maroon communities, sentiments of Pan-Negroism would emerge—the solidarity of all Africans, of all black men. Two goals began to take shape as to what *Black Power* should be used for: to return "home," to Africa; and to wrest the land where they toiled from the men who kept them in subjection—an extension of the Maroon pattern into *black nationalism.* Toussaint, Dessalines and Christophe, by 1804 had made the first conquest of New World soil by black men in the form of a nation-state.

Religion
in Afro-American Culture

The people of the Diaspora in North America never developed an *African-American* culture in the sense that the people of the Caribbean and South America did. Rather what might be called an *Afro*-American sub-culture evolved. Of the many factors that account for the difference—economic, demographic, and acculturational—perhaps the most important was the decision of the masters to encourage the Christianization of Africans as a means of social control to an extent that occurred nowhere else in the New World except in Barbados. Contemporary black nationalists speak of this scornfully as a "brain-washing," and the Black Muslims call upon Negroes to return to their "original religion"—Islam. In French, Spanish and Portuguese areas, the Latin-Catholic ethos resulted in religious syncretisms that permitted a viable African-American culture to develop. Although the need for more extensive research into the local sub-cultures exists, there is a large body of literature to documen: the process and its results.

The basic kinship unit of West African society was not preserved or reconstituted in the New World, the lineage that binds together brothers or sisters and their children and grandchildren into a tight-knit social group and which forms the basis of the ancestor-cult, the keystone of West African religion. However, the polygamous family or some variation of it persisted throughout the New World over a long span of time. With the disintegration of the lineage, religious beliefs and practices based upon the solidarity of a group of kinsmen did not become a part of the evolving African-American culture. The public cult centered upon traditional political rulers—chiefs, living and dead—was impossible to maintain in the New World setting except in Maroon communities, but a new public cult that gave social cohesion to individual black plantation communities developed in the Caribbean and South

America based upon integral parts of the more complex West African religious systems.

In Haiti and Brazil where the proportion of Dahomean and Yoruba slaves was high, the emerging Creole culture institutionalized the high status of two sets of holy persons, equally revered. There were priests and monks and nuns, predominantly white, who "knew" the Creator God in which all Africans already believed, and his sacrificed son about which the white man told them, but which fitted no religious concepts in their own societies. (Where human sacrifice did exist, outsiders, not kinsmen, were the victims.) But there were also black priests and priestesses who "knew" the other gods of Africa, including both those in the official pantheons who controlled rain and war and the smelting of iron, and the personal gods, *orishas* and *loas,* who, upon occasion entered into their bodies and transformed them into oracles, soothsayers and diviners. The songs and dances, the drumming and the sacrificial rites, were modified but preserved. In Haiti, the nature of the symbols and the rituals was misunderstood by white men and given the derogatory appellation of "voodoo;" without recognition of the fact that the "voodoo" priest or *houngan* became the most important temporal and spiritual leader on every plantation, and later, in every free peasant community. In Brazil, the priests and priestesses became leaders of Afro-Brazilian cults that existed side by side with the Catholic establishment, and in every city where black men reside in numbers they play a role even to this day.

In other areas of the New World, public religious rituals and functionaries in the African idiom disappeared, but the diviner-healer as well as the sorcerer became important personalities on the plantations and in the cities. What Africans today call "the juju man," West Indians, the "obeah man," and American Negroes, the "hoodoo man" performed the functions of allaying anxiety, assuring good luck, and of confounding enemies. And some of them were believed to have the power of wreaking destruction upon a client's enemies. (For reasons not entirely clear, however, the ubiquitous African phenomenon of the witch disappeared.) All such practitioners were defined as "agents of the Devil" by Christians, and traffic with them as a sin. New World Negroes continued to deal with them, however—or at least to believe in their powers—even when they became Christians.

Shirley Graham, in *There Was Once a Slave, The Heroic Story of Frederick Douglass,* recounts an episode that occurred in the 1830s which gives point to the fact of the persistence of beliefs in African magic and the ambivalence of those who had been Christianized toward them. Young Frederick Douglass is fleeing from a life of slavery, and the husband of the black family with whom he is hiding out is giving him advice:

Then Sandy reached inside the coarse shirt he was wearing and drew out a small pouch—something tied up in an old piece of cloth . . . Sandy extended the little bag . . . "Wear this close to body—all the time. No man ever beat you." Frederick's heart sank. He made no move to take the bag. His voice faltered. "But—but Sandy—that's voodoo. I don't believe in charms. I'm—I'm a Christian" . . . Sandy was very still . . . He spoke softly, "You be very young." He untied the little bag and carefully shook out its contents into the palm of his hand— dust, fine as powder, a bit of shriveled herb, and several smooth round pebbles. Then he held out the upturned hand to Frederick. "Look now," he said. "Soil of Africa—come cross the sea close to my mother's breast." Holding his breath Frederick bent his head. It was as if a great hand lay upon his heart. "And here"—Sandy's long fingers touched the withered fragment— "seaweed, flowered on great waters, waters of far off lands, waters of many lands." Holding Frederick's wrists, Sandy carefully emptied the bits on the boy's palm, then gently closed his fingers. "A thousand years of dust in one hand. Dust on men long gone, men who lived so you live. Your dust." He handed Frederick the little bag. And Frederick took it reverently. With the utmost care, lest one grain of dust be lost, he emptied his palm into it. Then drawing the cord tight, he placed the pouch inside his rags, fastening the cord securely. He stood up and his head was clear. Again the black man thought, *"He'll do"* . . . suddenly he (Frederick) knew that his life was important. He laid his hand on the black man's arm. "I won't be forgettin," he said. . . .

Douglass became one of America's great leaders of the Abolition Movement, but unlike many of his associates, he never displayed any special interest in Africa despite this episode that he relates in his autobiography.

The biased misconception that African religious customs are "just a mass of superstition" has been destroyed by careful modern scholarship. One British anthropologist, Meyer Fortes, in a perceptive essay on *Oedipus and Job* probed the philosophical basis of West African religious beliefs and provided a background for understanding the new religious systems that arose in African-American and Afro-American cultures in the New World. Janheinz Jahn performs a similar service in *Muntu*. The slaves brought with them the belief that their lives were controlled by Fate or Destiny, but that an individual, within the broad outlines of his predestined Fate could determine specific courses of action by consulting "diviners" and could take responsibility for his own affairs—a concept not far distant from that of Calvinistic theories of predestination, except that the "will of God" in Africa was not ascertained by individual prayer and "waiting on the Lord."

The belief in Divine Providence was grafted onto this African belief. However, concepts of sin and guilt that affected the afterlife of individuals or the destiny of groups did not exist in West African societies, and could offer no explanations of why people had been enslaved or what God or the gods had planned as the destiny of tribles and nations. Nevertheless, the trauma of The Diaspora forced reflection on these aspects of Man's Fate, and those slaves who became Christians were exposed to eschatological doctrines. In North America, where evangelical Protestantism of the Baptist and Methodist variety was deliberately taught to many of the slaves, a body of folk-music, the "spirituals," came into being which voiced the hope of an ultimate apocalyptic deliverance for the people of the Black Diaspora with the experience of the Jews as a paradigm: "Go Down Moses and Tell Old Pharaoh to Let My People Go,"—"My Lord Delivered Daniel. . . ." Pending deliverance for "the people," each individual would experience "deliverance" at death: "Swing Low Sweet Chariot, Coming for to Carry Me Home,"—"I Got Shoes, All God's Chillun Got Shoes, When I Get to Heaven Gonna Put on My Shoes." The concept of the Western African "high god" who did not interfere in human affairs was replaced by that of a God "who's got the whole world in his hands" and who, at the end of time, will judge all men:—"My Lord, What a Morning, When the Stars Begin to Fall!" This world of fantasy was articulated with a ritual that permitted great scope for emotional release and improvisation in word and act, unlike the structured ritual of West African ceremonies or of the Catholic Mass. Sorrow, loneliness, frustration, and hostility were dissolved in the catharsis of shouting and singing and in the ecstasy that some individuals experienced by possession of the Holy Ghost.

A study of the experience of black men in America gives vivid confirmation to the words that Karl Marx wrote, "Man makes religion. . . . Religion is the general theory of this world, its encyclopedic compendium, its logic in popular form, its spiritual *point d'honneur,* its enthusiasm, its moral sanction, its solemn complement, its general basis of consolation and justification. . . . Religious suffering is at the same time an expression of real suffering and a protest against real suffering. Religion is the sigh of the oppressed creature, the sentiment of a heartless world, and the soul of souless conditions. It is the opium of the people." But the slave's religion in the United States did not exhaust its content in the "sigh" of the spiritual or in orgiastic worship. It also produced currents of protest and action, similar to those "heresies" that fascinated Marx' associate, Engels, who emphasized the point that where religious thought-styles dominate an epoch, protest will be phrased in religious terms as well as the justifications for oppression and the escapist fantasies. Referring to the Utopian thought that led to peasant revolts in England and in Europe, Engels noted that "It demanded the restoration of early Christian equality . . . demands advanced with more or less determination as natural implications of the early Christian doctrine." The European inheritors of this tradition, the Quakers and Mennonites, were the first to challenge the system of slavery in the New World, but as early as 1774, the Governor of Massachusetts was presented with "The Petition of a Grate Number of Blacks of this Province who by divine permission are held in a state of slavery within the bowels of a free and Christian Country." The petitioners insisted that ". . . we have in common with all other men a natural right to our freedoms without being deprived of them by our fellowmen. . . . There is a great number of us sencear . . . members of the Church of Christ . . . Beare ye onenothers Bordenes How can the master be said to Beare my Borden when he Beares me down with the Have chanes of slavery and operson against my will . . . how can the slave perform the duties of a husband to a wife or parent to his child."

The note of protest is here and is accompanied by a petition: "We therfor Bage your Excellency and Honours will give its deer weight and consideration and that you will accordingly cause an act of the legislative to be passed that we may obtain our Natural right our freedoms and our children be set a lebety at the years of twenty one. . . ." The questioning had begun. The revolt was bound to come.

It is significant that this group of Christian slaves idealized the African "homeland" and did not perceive it as dark, benighted, and savage. In their petition they said, ". . . we were unjustly dragged by the cruel hand of power from our dearest frinds and sum of us stolen from the bosoms of our tender Parents and from a Populous Pleasant and plentiful country and Brought hither to be made slaves for Life in a Christian land." The year before this group of Christian slaves made their protest, Peter Estes, Sambo Freeman, Felix Holbrook and Chester Joie had sent forward a petition "In behalf of our fellow slaves in this province." They did not stress their devotion to Christianity and they stated explicitly that they wanted to go to Africa. They complimented the members of the legislature on their efforts to "free themselves from slavery," that is from English rule, and stated that "The divine spirit of *freedom* seems to fire every humane breast on this continent." They asked only that they be granted one day a week in which they could earn money to purchase their freedom, commenting that "Even the *Spaniards,* who have not the sublime ideas of freedom that English men have, are conscious that they have no right to all the services of their fellow men, we mean the *Africans.*" They promised to behave as long as they remained slaves "since the wise and righteous governor of the universe has permitted our fellow men to make us slaves" but asked that they be acted toward "by the *principles* of equity and justise," indicating a determination to leave the colony "as soon as we can, from our joint labours, procure money to transport ourselves to some part of the Coast of *Africa,* where we propose a settlement."

There is no way of knowing how many slaves thought of themselves as "sencear" Christians on the eve of the Revolutionary War or participated in Christian worship or shared in the values or believed the mythology expressed in the spirituals. There is some evidence, however, that the great majority of the slaves prior to 1776 were not Christians, and we know that black Christians continuously expressed concern over the activities of the "sinners" around them—their drinking and gambling, their dancing and singing of "worldly" songs, their sexuality outside of wedlock and their proneness to violence. Nor do we know how early the folk theology and ritual took form in North America and how prevalent it was prior to the Revolution.

The American Negro sociologist, E. Franklin Frazier, writing on "Christianity: A New Orientation Toward Existence" in *The Negro Church in America*, states that "Although slaves were regularly baptized and taken into the Anglican Church during the seventeenth century, it was not until the latter part of the eighteenth century that a systematic attempt was made on the part of the Church of England to Christianize Negroes in America. . . . Despite the reported success of the conversion of Negroes, a study of the situation revealed that only a small proportion of the slaves in the American colonies could be included even among nominal Christians . . . it was not until after the American Revolution that large masses of the Negro population became converts and joined the Methodist and Baptist churches. In the emotionalism of the camp meetings and revivals some social solidarity, even if temporary, was achieved and they. were drawn into a union with their fellow men." Negroes were participants in the religious movement that historians call "The Great Awakening" and which a scornful upper-class observer at the time said appealed mainly to "those of weak intellect and unstable emotions, women, adolescents, and Negroes." He omitted "poor whites."

Among the many circumstances that account for the large-scale conversion of Negroes after the Revolution is the fact that plantation communities had suffered considerable disorganization during the war and a general state of restlessness prevailed, and that among Negroes disillusionment and disappointment was widespread over the fact that while the colonies secured their freedom from Britain the blacks remained enslaved. The social situation was ripe for revivalism and the restoration of a sense of solidarity and hope. Out of this situation new leaders emerged—the Negro "elders," and "chair-backers," and "jack-leg preachers," who had a talent for oratory and singing, and occasionally some organizational skill. Neither the Baptist or Methodist church demanded any training for its ministers. All that was necessary was the conviction of a "call." Intelligent and ambitious individuals now found a new role in the American social system and some of them won prestige in a community of "the saved" that cut across racial lines. Lemuel Haynes, for instance, became a powerful speaker, preaching to white congregations within 20 years after the American Revolution ended. Even in the South, Negroes preached to mixed congregations during "The Great Awakening," but the post-Revolution Pentecostal outburst was not powerful enough to break the barriers of class and caste—nor would the slaveholders allow it. In neither the North or South were Negroes and whites knit together into unsegregated Christian congregations. A "Negro church" came into being.

Two types of Negro congregations arose, one being what Frazier calls "the invisible institution," those congregations on the plantations presided over by illiterate or semi-literate slaves who functioned as part-time preachers and who developed a style of exhortation and interpretation that gives color and gusto to the Negro church even today. The other was the church led by urban Free Negroes who were often literate, though unschooled, Frazier's "institutional church," with theology and ritual more orthodox and patterned on that of white denominations. To some extent this was a "protest" church led by men who had met rebuffs or blockage of opportunity in white congregations. They conceived of themselves as leaders of those masses, however, who from the outset had no problems of identity as the names of their churches indicate: First *African* Baptist Church, Savannah, Georgia (1788); *African* Baptist Church, Lexington, Kentucky (1790); *Abyssinia* Baptist Church, New York City (1800); Free *African* Meeting House, Boston (1805); First *African* Presbyterian Church, Philadelphia (1807); First *African* Baptist Church, Philadelphia (1809); Union Church of *Africans,* Wilmington (1813); First *African* Baptist Church, New Orleans (1826); First *African* Baptist Church, Richmond, Virginia (1841). Free African Societies with both religious and mutual benefit functions were organized between 1787 and 1810 in Newport, Rhode Island, Philadelphia, Boston and New York. Neither slaves nor freedmen had been accepted as "Americans" despite the egalitarian sentiments in the Declaration of Independence, so they proudly called themselves, *African!*

During the fifty years between 1780 and 1830 when Christianity was spreading rapidly among American Negroes, their religious leaders could not avoid taking a stand on the question of slavery. The spirituals reflected the objective fact of mass non-resistance by both believers and unbelievers, but provided a theological rationale for acceptance of low status for those who were believers. The idea of patient suffering without overt rebellion until deliverance for the individual came through death, and for the group when God was ready to show his hand, was given a more sophisticated expression than that found in the spirituals by an occasional slave who was fortunate enough to secure some education. Jupiter Hammond, who lived in New York between 1720 and 1800, is usually referred to as the first American Negro poet. Never, himself, expressing a desire for emancipation by the master who had been kind to him, he wrote a note of advice to his fellow slaves at the age of 70, reinforcing what nearly all white Christians, North and South, were saying to black men:

> "I think you will be more likely to listen to what is said when you know it comes from a Negro, one of your own nation and colour . . . I am now upwards of seventy years old . . . I am certain that while we are slaves, it is our duty to obey our masters in all their lawful commands and mind them unless we are bid to do that which we know to be sin, or forbidden in God's word. . . . Now I acknowledge that liberty is a great thing, and worth seeking for if we can get it honestly. . . . *That liberty is a great thing we may know from our own feelings, and we may likewise judge so from the conduct of the white people in the late war. I must say that I have hoped that God would open their eyes, when they were so much engaged for liberty, to think of the state of the poor blacks and pity us.* . . . Let me beg of you, my dear African brethren, to think very little of your bondage in this life; for your thinking of it will do you no good. If God designs to set us free, he will do it in his own time and way; but think of your bondage to sin and Satan, and do not rest until you are delivered from it. . . ."

27

These sentiments were also echoed by Phyllis Wheatley, who had been bought at the age of six or seven by a well-to-do Boston family and was taught to read and write by her master and mistress. When they found she had a gift for writing poetry they encouraged her. She is best known perhaps for a laudatory poem she wrote to George Washington and for Thomas Jefferson's comment on how bad her poetry was. She not only was preoccupied with the subject of personal salvation, but also, in a letter to a girl who, it is thought, had been a "shipmate" on the Middle Passage, revealed attitudes toward Africa quite different from those of the semi-literate petitioners who asked the Massachusetts Legislature for their freedom:

> "Let us rejoice in and adore the wonders of God's infinite love in bringing us from a land semblant of darkness itself, and where the divine light of revelation (being obscured) is in darkness. Here the knowledge of the true God and eternal life are made manifest; but there was nothing in us to recommend us to God. . . ."

That these two poets who owed their privileged status in life to kind Northern masters reacted as they did is not surprising. The leaders of Negro congregations were a different breed of men, however. While some were the beneficiaries of kind masters, others were men who had run away or bought their freedom. Their contacts were with their own people and their livelihood depended upon their allegiance. They knew that some black men had fought on both sides during the Revolution and gained their freedom thereby. Most of them were disappointed, as Jupiter Hammond was, that the sentiments expressed in the Declaration of Independence had not been extended to black men. Beginning in 1789, they followed events in Haiti with great interest and were aware of the fact that many black men in the seaports—Philadelphia, Washington, Baltimore, Charleston, Savannah and New Orleans, were absorbing the details and the rumors of the great Caribbean revolt from sailors and white refugees. As leaders they felt a responsibility to give guidance during this critical period, and as members of an emerging black middle-class they favored "law and order" and stressed "moral uplift" for the poor blacks, both slave and free. The Haitian revolution posed a problem for them.

There was no group of leaders anywhere in the Caribbean during the second half of the 18th Century equivalent to the preachers among the American Negroes. In the French and Spanish areas there were no black Christian religious leaders at all. The priests were white. San Domingo, the most prosperous island in the West Indies was divided between the French and the Spanish, and the French Revolution had thrown the French section into turmoil. Unlike the situation in the United States, free men of color stood completely aloof from the black slaves, supplying no leadership for them, but organizing to protect their own interests. In 1791, the blacks of Haiti rose up against both the whites and the free persons of color and a 12-year armed struggle began that ended with the proclamation of the Republic of Haiti in 1804. C. L. R. James, in *The Black Jacobins* presents a vivid reconstruction of the beginning of the insurrection, revealing the role of religion in the rebellion: ". . . the rising was . . . a thoroughly prepared and organized mass movement. . . . Voodoo was the medium of the conspiracy. In spite of all the prohibitions, the slaves had traveled miles to sing and dance and practice the rites and talk; and, now, since the revolution (in France) to hear the political news and make their plans. Boukman, a Papaloi or High Priest, a gigantic Negro, was the leader. . . . One night the slaves in the suburbs and outskirts of LeCap were to fire the plantations. At this signal the slaves in the town would massacre the whites and the slaves on the plain would complete the destruction. . . . That so vast a conspiracy was not discovered until it had actually broken out is a testimony to their solidarity. . . ."

"On the night of the 22nd of August 1791, a tropical storm raged, with lightning and gusts of wind and heavy showers of rain. . . . Boukman gave the last instructions and, after Voodoo incantations and the sucking of the blood of a stuck pig, he stimulated his followers by a prayer spoken in Creole '. . . the god who created the sun which gives us light, who rouses the waves and rules the storm, though hidden in the clouds he watches us. . . . Our god who is good to us orders us to avenge our wrongs. He will direct our arms and aid us. Throw away the symbol of the god of the whites who has so often caused us to weep, and listen to the voice of liberty, which speaks in the hearts of us all.' The symbol of the god

29

of the whites was the cross, which, as Catholics, they wore round their necks. That very night they began. . . ."

One month after the insurrection started, a 45-year old slave who took his Catholicism seriously, as well as the promises of the French revolutionaries, made a fateful decision. He was a coachman for a master who respected him for his intelligence and diligence, the slave having learned to read and write. However, the master did not know that he was poring over Caesar's *Commentaries* and Abbe Reynal's books on the West Indies and East Indies. He was held in high esteem among the slaves, too, but when the insurrection broke out he decided to remain with his master and mistress and protect their property and their lives. At last. however, he felt the time had come to send the master and mistress away to safety as well as his own family. Then, having done so, he made his way to the camp of the rebels and joined the revolution. The French were throwing all of their military might at the ragged rebels and forcing them to the hills. He quickly sized up the situation and took a band of slaves into Spanish territory across the border and drilled them into an army. And then, in August, 1793, believing that God had appointed him to do so, he took charge of the revolt. With an army of 5,000 men he approached the border of the French territory and sent a message across to his people:

"Brothers and friends. I am Toussaint L'Ouverture, my name is perhaps known to you. I have undertaken vengeance. I want Liberty and Equality to reign in San Domingo. I work to bring them into existence. Unite yourselves to us, brothers, and fight with us for the same cause."

The words were spoken to Toussaint's black brothers in Haiti but they leaped the ocean and reverberated along the eastern seaboard of the United States. It did not escape the attention of literate Negroes that within a year the United States government was dealing with this black man as an equal and that American merchants were supplying him with the sinews of war when he had to fight off the French invading armies. However, whatever admiration they may have had for Toussaint L'Ouverture, and however great the vicarious enjoyment of witnessing a black general putting white armies to flight, the sobering fact had to be faced that what a black majority could do on the island of Haiti was quite different from what a black minority embedded in the heart of a large white nation could realistically hope for.

When Dessalines established the black republic of Haiti in 1804 it was a harbinger of hope to American Negroes as well as to West Indians, though precisely what its effects would, or could be, no one knew. These hopes were articulated by one of the most prominent leaders of the period, a well-to-do Barbadian immigrant who lived in Cambridge, Massachusetts where he had established a school for colored children. In 1787, when the American Masonic lodge refused an application of Negroes for a charter, he had secured one from the Grand Lodge of Ireland, and founded the first fraternal order among Afro-Americans, African Lodge No. 459, with himself, Prince Hall, its founder, as Grand Master. In a speech on "The Duty of a Mason to a Mason, and Charity and Love to All Mankind," he detailed the sufferings of black men in the United States, and then said, *"My brethren, let us remember what a dark day it was with our African brethren, six years ago in the French West Indies. . . . But blessed be God the scene is changed. . . ."*

Prince Hall was a preacher, but not all of his fellow ministers were prepared to praise Toussaint who said, "I have undertaken vengeance," (although he actually extended generosity to his beaten foes) and certainly not to his successor, Dessalines, who after Toussaint had been betrayed by the French, took power with the cry, "Death to all Frenchmen!"

One of the most influential preachers among the Afro-Americans was Richard Allen. In 1791, while Boukman, the Papaloi, was preparing the blacks of Haiti, through the medium of the voodoo ritual for revolt, and the drums were calling the sons of Africa to strike for Black Power, Allen had a different task. A Negro who had bought his freedom, he was now diligently recruiting members in Philadelphia for the Free African Society that he and Absalom Jones had founded when they were attacked physically in the white St. George Methodist Episcopal Church for sitting in pews reserved for white people. Allen was a Methodist preacher. By 1816, he had become the leading Negro minister in the United States and was organizing the first all-black denomination in the country, one that would eventually number its adherents in the millions—the African Methodist Episcopal Church (A.M.E.). Within 70 years its mis-

31

sionaries would be under attack in South Africa for fomenting rebellion among the blacks, but its founder, soon after the insurrection in Haiti, was advising the slaves to accept their position in life.

He first addressed an appeal "To Those Who Keep Slaves and Approve the Practice," stating, "I do not wish to make you angry, but excite your attention to consider how hateful slavery is in the sight of God who hath destroyed kings and their princes for their oppression of the poor slaves." Commenting upon American Negroes, he said:

"I will also show why they appear contented as they can in your sight, but *the dreadful insurrections they have made when opportunity has offered is enough to convince a reasonable man that great uneasiness and not contentment is the inhabitant of their hearts.* God himself hath pleaded their cause; He hath from time to time raised up instruments for that purpose sometimes mean and contemptible in your sight, at other times He hath used such as it hath pleased him, with whom you have not thought it beneath your dignity to contend."

Having warned the slave-holders, he then addressed a message "To the People of Color." Allen's tone was in marked contrast to that of the West Indian, Prince Hall, who had seen hope for freedom in Haiti: His advice was that of Jupiter Hammond and Phyllis Wheatley:

". . . as your hearts are inclined to serve God, you will feel an affectionate regard towards your masters and mistresses, so called, and the whole family in which you live. This will be seen by them and tend to promote your liberty, especially with such as have feeling masters; and if they are otherwise, you will have the favor and love of God dwelling in your hearts . . . life is short and uncertain, and the chief end of our having a being in this world is to be prepared to a better. I wish you to think more of this than anything else . . . and if the trouble of your condition ends with your lives you will be admitted to the freedom which God hath prepared for those of all colors that love him. Here the power of the most cruel masters ends, and all sorrows and tears are wiped away."

Another eloquent minister, William Whipper, added a dimension of hope that both he and Richard Allen shared, but also with an appeal for nonviolence:

"Vengeance is mine saith the Lord. . . . If, amid these difficulties, we can but possess our souls in patience we shall finally triumph over our enemies. . . . Whoever for any cause inflicts a single blow on a fellow human being violates the laws of God and of his country and has no just claim to being regarded as a Christian or a good citizen."

Allen and Whipper, not Prince Hall, represented the dominant view among the educated Negro clergy during the opening years of the 19th Century. Viewed from the perspective of a century later, what they have to say sounds unusually passive and accommodative. Put within the context of the period, however, a case could be made for the caution—and perhaps the hope—of those who defined their role as "wise" leaders, even if a case cannot be made either for their other-worldly orientation or for their reading of the future.

Richard Allen and the religious leaders who shared his views were convinced that forces at work that would bring the end of slavery without violent insurrection. By 1800, all of the Northern states had abolished slavery through legislative action. Antislavery forces were being mobilized by the Quakers and various humanitarian groups in the North. There were hopeful signs in the South, too, since George Washington, Thomas Jefferson, and other slaveholders who had led the revolt against Britain felt embarrassed and guilty over the compromises that were made with the states of the deep south in order to hammer out a constitution for the newly formed United States of America. They became leaders in the movement for manumission or voluntary emancipation and, themselves, set the example. On December 29, 1799, Richard Allen gave an address on the death of George Washington, commenting that "To us he has been the sympathizing friend and tender father. . . . Unbiased by the popular opinion of the state in which is the memorable Mt. Vernon, he dared do his duty and wipe off the only stain with which man could ever reproach him. . . . The bread of oppression was not sweet to his taste, and he 'let the oppressed go free! . . . that those who had been slaves might rejoice in the day of their deliverance." This optimism about the possibility of widespread voluntary emancipation was reinforced by a belief that fear of slave revolts would stimulate others to free their slaves from considerations of prudence. Allen saw the "dreadful insurrections" as wrong, but also as "a case in which God uses the wrath of men to praise him" and out of evil comes forth some good. Aside from this effect, however—and there was doubt as to how much good insurrections really did bring—increased suppression followed the abortive revolts, including bans on worship without the presence of whites. Granted the heroism of the black martyrs, were not the deaths of these leaders and the subsequent reprisals too great a price to pay? Insurrections in the United States could not result in the founding of a black nation as in Haiti. Even if not betrayed by other slaves, as so many of them were, how could the leaders of revolts ever hope to succeed? And what, indeed, was success? What were the goals other than vengeance?

When Richard Allen reminded the slaveholders of "dreadful insurrections" he knew that all of them were still nervous over a recent incident. In 1800, an extensive plot was discovered in Virginia, when two slaves informed their masters of their impending doom. One stormy night in August ". . . at least one thousand slaves had appeared at their agreed rendezvous, six miles outside Richmond, armed with swords and clubs, but could not advance because of the flood." The next day the whites having been warned, scores of slaves were arrested. The leader, Gabriel Prosser, had planned well and with discrimination. His followers were under orders to spare all women, Methodists, Quakers, and Frenchmen. Poor-whites and Catawba Indians were expected to join the revolt. But the results were disastrous. A lawyer present at the trial told an English visitor that one of the insurrectionists, when asked what he had to say, replied,

> "I have nothing more to offer than what General Washington would have had to offer, had he been taken by the British officers and put to trial by them. I have ventured my life in endeavouring to obtain the liberty of my countrymen, and I am a willing sacrifice to their cause; and I beg as a favor, that I may be immediately led to execution. I know that you have predetermined to shed my blood; why then this mockery of a trial?"

Virginia's Governor, James Monroe, who interviewed Gabriel, reported that "From what he said to me, he seemed to have made up his mind to die, and to have resolved to say but little on the subject of the conspiracy." Thomas Jefferson pleaded for clemency, pointing out that ". . . other states in the world at large will forever condemn us if we indulge in a principle of revenge or go one step beyond absolute necessity." Gabriel was executed along with 35 of his rebel band.

Thomas Jefferson saw these attempts at insurrection as an 18th century libertarian Deist would—the efforts of men because they *were* men to strike off their chains—and he warned the Virginia legislature that though they, of necessity, viewed the slaves' action as criminal, neither the Negroes nor many of their white sympathizers made this appraisal. Robert Allen, on the other hand, as a Methodist preacher, saw the attempts to revolt as un-Christian acts of violence, but functioning as a warning from God to slaveholders to repent, *i.e.,* to free their slaves. Both Jefferson and Allen were aware that slave plots did not begin with Gabriel. They may not have known what historian Aptheker's careful research later revealed, that there had been 42 major conspiracies and revolts between 1663 and 1776, including two attempts to burn down New York City but they were vividly aware that during the very month that the Founding Fathers were drafting the Declaration of Independence, a plot was uncovered in South Carolina and put down with great severity; and that, after the Revolutionary War, some slaves, dissatisfied because the victory over Britain had not brought them their freedom, had insurrection on the mind. Herbert Aptheker, in his pioneering study of *Negro Slave Revolts in the United States: 1526-1860* comments on the prevalence of slave conspiracies in Virginia, North Carolina, and Louisiana during 1791 and 1792, which was a period of economic distress in the South. He states that "Many hundreds of slaves were implicated, scores were jailed, dozens lashed and several executed." During the next year a number of alleged plots were discovered in Virginia, and a citizen of Richmond, Virginia claimed to have overheard three slaves discussing a plot in which "The one who seemed to be the chief speaker said 'You see how the blacks has killed the whites in the French island (San Domingo) and took it awhile ago?'" The white reaction in Virginia was ". . . mobilization and arming of the militias of the affected areas, the arrest of scores of slaves and the torture and execution of the rebel leaders." In 1795, in Louisiana, which was still a Spanish colony, a plot was discovered in which at least three whites were implicated along with the Negroes. The army was called out; ". . . the slaves resisted arrest and twenty-five of them were killed. Twenty-three others were executed, and the bodies of nine of these were left hanging near the churches of the region. Many others were severely lashed. . . ."

Four years after the Gabriel plot was foiled, Dessalines proclaimed Haiti an independent state. The news spread from the North American ports where it was brought by seamen and white refugees into the backlands. The South was thrown into a state of anxiety verging upon hysteria. Black nationalism now loomed as a spectre rather than mere sporadic revolts. During the next twenty years Virginia experienced 13 revolts, and Thomas Jefferson believed that events in Haiti had been a factor in setting them off. There were at least 19 in Maryland, Tennessee, North Carolina, Kentucky, South Carolina, Florida, Georgia, and Mississippi, as well as five in Louisiana. In 1810, for instance, a plan for revolt seemed to be shaping up involving slaves in Virginia and North Carolina, with ramifications extending as far southward as Georgia where one white citizen wrote to another, "The most vigorous measures are being taken to defeat their infernal designs. May God preserve us from the fate of St. Domingo." An actual revolt broke out in Louisiana in 1811 reputedly led by "a free mulatto from St. Domingo" in which the slaves began to march from plantation to plantation with drums beating and flags flying. A full scale army assault was unleashed against them. The militia had to be called out in New Orleans the next year to guard against a plot. Then, in 1816, a white man, Boxley, attempted to lead a slave revolt in Virginia but was betrayed by a Negro woman. Six slaves were hanged and six banished but the white leader escaped. Later that same year Camden, South Carolina hanged six Negroes accused of plotting a rising, and two major expeditions were carried out against "maroon" groups in Florida and South Carolina. In 1822, eighteen years after Haiti became a sovereign state, a conspiracy was uncovered in Charleston, South Carolina that Aptheker describes as ". . . one of the most, if not the most, extensive in American history." The leader was a West Indian, Denmark Vesey, who had purchased his freedom with winnings from a lottery ticket, although he had not been able to obtain freedom for his wife and children.

It was recorded at Vesey's trial that local slaveowners had urged him to emigrate to Africa, but he said he would not "because he had not the will, he wanted to stay and see what he could do for his fellow creatures." He studied the anti-slavery speeches made in Congress when the Missouri question was being debated. He also questioned everyone he could about what was happening in Haiti and is said to have actually sent two letters to the leaders of that black nation seeking active aid in the Charleston conspiracy. Denmark Vesey set to work organizing fighting units based on tribal identity among the few groups in Charleston that remembered their origins and he used an Angola diviner named Gullah Jack to administer oaths to them and to assure them of their invulnerability to harm. Vesey himself, however, read the Bible to his followers, assuring them of freedom just as ". . . the children of Israel were delivered out of Egypt from Bondage." Between 6,000 and 9,000 blacks from Charleston and its surroundings were drawn into the plot. Two hundred and fifty pike heads were manufactured and over 300 daggers. Every store containing arms had been marked for capture. Simultaneous attacks on Charleston were to be made from five points and a sixth band was to collect horses from the plantations and to patrol the Charleston streets. The date was set for a Sunday in July, but a house servant betrayed the plans. Gabriel ordered his lieutenants to "Die silent as you shall see me do."

One hundred and thirty-one Negroes were arrested in Charleston and forty-seven were condemned. Twelve were pardoned and deported, but thirty-five were hanged. Some were acquitted. Four white men—American, Scottish, Spanish, German—were fined and imprisoned for encouraging the slaves to revolt. While the insurrectionaries were awaiting trial word got around that groups of slaves were planning to rescue them from prison, and one actual attempt was made, but quickly suppressed. Repression in Charleston did not end conspiracy and plotting either there or elsewhere in the United States.

Aptheker reports that "From 1821 through 1831, there were incessant reports of slave unrest throughout the South" and relates the restlessness to the fact that ". . . Southern papers were filled with praise for revolutionists in Turkey, Greece, Italy, Spain, France,

Belgium, Poland, South America, the West Indies and Mexico. . . . Slave uprisings in Brazil, Venezuela, Martinique, Puerto Rico, Cuba, Antigua, Tortola and Jamaica also found ther way into the local press and conversation." Mexico abolished slavery in 1829 and there was an upsurge in the anti-slavery movement in Britain. It was impossible to isolate even illiterate slaves from the news of these events, and literates among the urban Negroes discussed them continuously. During the decade after the Denmark Vesey conspiracy, five more attempts at insurrection were uncovered in South Carolina, 13 in Virginia, 5 each in North Carolina and Louisiana, 4 in Georgia, and one or two each in Pennsylvania, Maryland, Kentucky, Tennessee, Florida and Mississippi. In 1826, 29 slaves aboard a slave ship, the *Decatur,* revolted, killed the captain, and ordered one of the other officers to take them to Haiti. The boat was captured and they were taken to New York where all of them escaped except one who was executed. Three years later, a similar revolt took place on the *Lafayette* that was transporting slaves from New Orleans to Virginia, and they, too, gave orders, "Sail to Haiti!" but were subdued!

Early in 1831, at the request of the local authorities the United States government sent two companies of infantry to New Orleans and five to Fort Monroe on the seacoast in Virginia. But the insurrection that the fearful expected was gestating elsewhere. A sensitive and gifted slave on a plantation near Southampton, Virginia, Nat Turner, had selected four trusted friends, and, together, they were planning a day of reckoning. This slave had taught himself to read and write and both white men and black praised him for his skill in making pottery and gunpowder, and even paper. He was considered a "moral" man who never swore or drank and would never steal. He had taught himself to read and write, and after much prayer and fasting and Bible reading felt the "call" and became a Baptist preacher. He was highly esteemed among his fellow slaves and they held him in awe because he was reputed to dream dreams and see visions and hear voices. There were certain visions however, that he confided only to his closest associates—the ". . . white spirits and black spirits contending in the skies" while "the sun was darkened and the thunder rolled." He brooded over slavery and over the 16 attempted slave revolts in his own state during his lifetime, the fate of Denmark Vesey, and what he had heard of things hap-

38

pening on plantations throughout the South during the last few years. He studied his Bible for guidance and prayed.

The contradictions in the Bible and within his own mind were not solved so simply and easily as they were by northern free Negro preachers such as Richard Allen. At first Nat Turner was convinced that the Bible meant all men to be free and he ran away in 1826. But doubts assailed him and he came back, feeling, as he phrased it, that "I should return to the service of my earthly master." Then the slaves "found fault and murmured against me, saying that if they had my sense they would not serve any master in the world." Nat Turner began to search his Bible and his soul and his inner tension was broken one day in 1828 while he was ploughing when he had an overwhelming conviction "that he was to take up *Christ's* struggle for the oppressed, 'for the time was fast approaching when the first should be last and the last should be first.'" After three years of prayer and fasting and confirming visions, he picked his men.

When the solar eclipse of February 12, 1831 occurred, Nat Turner was convinced that this was God's sign for the "work" to begin. He invited his trusted followers to come to a meeting and he told them that the day was drawing near. They set it for July 4, at a time when white men would be celebrating their decision to be free from Britain, but Nat Turner was sick that day. Another sign came on August 13, when the sun had a peculiar color. Nat called his men to meet him on the following Sunday, August 21. There was no African ritual and the administration of an oath as on the day that Boukman prepared to strike in Haiti. Under the guise of a barbecue there was only quiet talk and prayer. They decided that God wanted them to strike that night. The objective was to free all the slaves in the county and to take over control of the area, and as Turner later explained it, "It was agreed that we should commence at home on that night, and until we had armed and equipped ourselves and gained sufficient force, neither age nor sex was to be spared; which was invariably adhered to." (There was no violation of the women, as in Haiti, however.)

They began with Nat Turner's master and his entire family and within 24 hours the band of avengers had grown to 70, some on horses, and 60 people were dead—every white person in a 20-square mile area except one family of poor whites who held no slaves. They were deliberately spared. The slaves gathered arms as they went, and planned to take the arsenal in the county courthouse, but a fatal miscalculation in their timing brought on a posse and the militia before they were fully armed. As a result of two pitched battles their ranks were broken and Turner went into hiding waiting for his men to regroup and come to him. They never came. For two months he eluded pursuit by hiding in a cave. Then, one day he was caught. When the counsel assigned to him asked whether he "still believed in his own Providential mission," he answered simply, "Was not Christ crucified?" It was reported that "He met his death with perfect composure, declined addressing the multitude assembled, and told the sheriff in a firm voice that he was ready. . . ." The rope ended his life. Nat Turner, who was called "Old Prophet Nat" by the slaves was a very different type of preacher from either Prince Hall or Richard Allen.

God's Hand in Black History

The ten years between the Denmark Vesey Conspiracy and the Nat Turner Revolt were among the most important in the history of the Negro in the United States. A well-financed "colonization movement" emerged, designed to encourage free Negroes to leave the United States. It was one aspect of the manumission movement for which Thomas Jefferson was the most persuasive spokesman. He took the position that slaves had every right to use insurrectionary violence to free themselves and that the various plots and insurrections indicated that black men in America would increasingly resort to such means. Prudent men would not wait to have their throats cut; they would free their slaves voluntarily. He believed, however, that black men and white men could never exist in peace or as equals in the same society, and was, therefore, in favor of providing training for them and assisting them to emigrate outside of the boundaries of the United States, either to the Far West, or to the Caribbean, or to Africa. Many southern slaveholders who were not manumissionists were disturbed over the presence of the freedmen who were already concentrated in southern cities and wanted to see them "deported;" others were embarrassed by the presence of the evidence of their miscegenation always around them.

Colonization societies had come into being in Virginia and Maryland by 1800 and were in contact with the British humanitaians who had sponsored a settlement at Freetown in Sierra Leone. They found allies among a group of Quakers and other anti-slavery leaders in the North whose motivations were quite different, who wanted to see American Negroes going to Africa as teachers and missionaries, and who elaborated the doctrine of "Providential Design" to give sanction to their plans—"*God, in his inscrutable way, had allowed Africans to be carried off into slavery so that they could be Christianized and civilized and return to uplift their kinsmen in Africa.*" As one Catholic father eloquently phrased it:

41

"The branch torn away from the parent stem in Africa, by our ancestors, was brought to American—brought away by Divine permission, in order that it might be engrafted upon the tree of the Cross. It will return in part to its own soil, not by violence or deportation, but willingly, and borne on the wings of faith and charity."

The American Colonization Society was founded in 1817 and the first load of immigrants left on an American naval vessel in 1882. The president of the society was George Washington's brother, General Bushrod Washington. The settlement was eventually called Monrovia in honor of Virginia's former Governor, President Monroe.

The colonization movement split the Afro-American leadership group. Some were in favor of co-operation with the white colonizationists in order to achieve "Black Power" goals. As early as 1808, a prosperous Negro shipowner in Boston, bearing a West African name, Paul Cuffee (i.e., Kofi), had begun to study the reports of the settlement of black people at Freetown, Sierra Leone, where some of the slaves who had deserted to the British during the Revolutionary War were taken. He became convinced that a program of selective immigration of American Negro freedmen should be instituted to supply leadership to the 2,000 black people already settled in Africa and the thousands that would be landed by British naval vessels as they captured slave ships on the high seas in the attempt to stop the trans-Atlantic slave trade. He visualized an intensive program of education that would lead eventually to the rise of new sovereign states in West Africa, and foresaw ". . . a vast trade between Negro America and West Africa designed to enhance the wealth and prestige of the race." He made a trip to Sierra Leone in his own boat in 1811, and four years later he carried over 38 settlers at his own expense. For a while he was in favor of co-operating with white colonizationists, but then later he refused to do so.

Paul Cuffee reinforced "emigrationist" tendencies among Negroes that never died out, but fluctuated in strength with the rise and fall of economic and social conditions. These were the voluntary, self-financed efforts of Negroes to settle in Africa. Some emigrationists had no uplift ideology but were simply trying to escape

42

from what they felt were intolerable conditions in the U.S.A. The first Negro college graduate in the U.S., the editor of the first Negro newspaper, John Russworm, abandoned his *Freedom's Journal* in 1829, two years after he founded it and left for Liberia. Most of the Negro leaders, however, took the position that black men should stay in the U.S. and fight for their rights, and repudiating the name, "African," for their organizations, began to organize *Colored Men's* Conventions. This was not abandonment of interest in Africa, but they felt that to continue to call themselves "African," now, was an invitation to deportation.

In 1829, the year that the editor of *Freedom's Journal* emigrated to Africa, a publication appeared that created consternation in the South. A free Negro, born in North Carolina, but living in Boston, published what he called *David Walker's Appeal to the Coloured Citizens of the World, but in Particular and Very Expressly, to Those of the United States of America.* It was rumored that white citizens in the South immediately placed a price of $3,000 on his head, and a year after Walker published the *Appeal* he was found mysteriously dead in the streets of Boston. Walker had been an agent for *Freedom's Journal* and was disturbed at the "defection" of its editor to Liberia. One of the four chapters in his booklet was on "Our Wretchedness in Consequence of the Colonizing Scheme." Denouncing it as a trick and a plot, he quoted with approval from an article written by Richard Allen who had said, "Why should they send us into a far country to die? See the thousands of foreigners emigrating to America every year: and if there be ground sufficient for them to cultivate and bread for them to eat, why would they wish to send the first tillers of the land away? Africans have made fortunes for thousands, who are yet unwilling to part with their services; but the free must be sent away and those who remain, must be slaves. I have no doubt that there are many good men who do not see as I do, and who are for sending us to Liberia; but they have not duly considered the subject—they are not men of colour. This land which we have watered with our tears and our blood, is now our mother country, and we are well satisfied to stay where wisdom abounds and the gospel is free."

Although David Walker lauded Richard Allen in the article, its general tone was very different from Allen's. He hinted at a coming insurrection, ". . . I am one of the oppressed, degraded and wretched sons of Africa, rendered so by the avaricious and unmerciful among the whites . . . know ye that I am in the hand of God, and at your disposal. . . . But remember Americans, that, as miserable, wretched, degraded and abject as you have made us . . . some of you (whites) on the continent of America will yet curse the day that you were ever born. . . . My colour will yet root some of you out of the very face of the earth!!!!! O! save us, we pray thee, thou God of Heaven and of earth, from the devouring hand of the white Christians!!!!"

David Walker, speaking to "My dearly beloved Brethren and Fellow Citizens" was summoning them to stick together so that they could act effectively to "root out" the oppressors. He assailed ". . . some of my brethren in league with the tyrants, selling their own brethren into hell on earth" by acting as spies and informers and counseling acquiescence in slavery. He spoke glowingly of the revolt in Haiti and commented that, "The whites have had us under them for more than three centuries, murdering and treating us like brutes . . . they do not know indeed that there is an uncontrollable disposition in the breasts of the blacks, which, when it is fully awakened and put in motion, will be subdued only with the destruction of the animal existence. Get the blacks started, and if you do not have a gang of tigers and lions to deal with them, I am a deceiver of the blacks and of the whites." Although counseling education, piety and faith, what he called for most vigorously was racial solidarity, "O! that the coloured people were long since of Moses' excellent disposition, instead of courting favour with, and telling news and lies to our *natural enemies,* against each other—aiding them to keep their hellish chains of slavery upon us. Would we not long before this time have been respectable men, instead of such wretched victims of oppression as we are? . . . The question, my brethren, I leave for you to digest; and may God almighty force it home to your hearts. Remember that unless you are united, keeping your tongues within your teeth, you will be afraid to trust your secrets to each other and thus perpetuate our miseries under the Christians!!!! . . . Never make an attempt to gain our freedom or *natural right* from under our cruel oppressors and murderers, until you see your way clear—when that hour arrives and you move, be not afraid or dismayed; for be you assured that Jesus

44

Christ the king of heaven and of earth and who is the God of Justice and of armies will go before you. . . ."

Walker had faith in the power of the written word to stir his people, writing in the preface to his last edition:

"It is expected that all coloured men, women and children, of every nation, language and tongue under heaven, will try to procure a copy of this *Appeal* and read it, or get some one to read it to them. . . . Let them remember that though our cruel oppressors and murderers, may (if possible) treat us more cruel, as Pharaoh did the children of Israel, *yet the God of the Ethiopians, has been pleased to hear our moans in consequence of oppression and the day our redemption from abject wretchedness draweth near, when we shall be enabled in the most extended sense of the word, to stretch our hands to the Lord our God. . . .*"

To Walker, the God he served was "the God of the Ethiopians."

When Nat Turner brought down a Day of Wrath upon Southampton County, there was a widespread tendency to blame Walker's agitation for his act, as well as for other disturbances throughout the South. The *Appeal,* and what was interpreted as Walker's martyrdom, probably had its greatest influence, however, among educated freedmen in the North, moving a larger number of them in the direction of sanctioning violence.

In 1833, slavery was abolished in the British Empire. Hope for abolition in America burgeoned, and that same year the American Anti-Slavery Society was founded, supporting a two-pronged program: an Underground Railroad for helping as many slaves as possible to steal away to the North, and the mobilizing of support for a political solution by electing candidates of a national party committed to the abolition of slavery. During the next thirty years the national crisis deepened, building up toward what has been called "The Irrepressible Conflict."

Some Northern Negroes felt that the Underground Railroad helped individuals but could not operate on such a massive scale as to destroy the slave system. They believed that the slaves must revolt. Three years after Nat Turner's death, a highly educated Northern free Negro Presbyterian preacher, Henry Highland Garnet, speaking before a national convention of coloured leaders in 1843, sounded a call for revolt:

> "Brethren, arise, arise! Strike for your lives and liberties. Now is the day and the hour. Let every slave throughout the land do this, and the days of slavery are numbered. You cannot be more oppressed than you have been—you cannot suffer greater cruelties than you have already. *Rather* die freemen than live to be slaves. Remember that you are FOUR MILLIONS! . . . In the name of God, we ask, are you men? Where is the blood of your fathers? Has it all run out of your veins? Awake, awake. . . . Let your motto be resistance! resistance! RESISTANCE!"

A resolution of support for this policy lost by only one vote, but those who would have to pay the price did not respond. In fact insurrectionary plotting diminished as the Underground Railroad became more efficient. The most militant slaves went North, and spirituals such as "Steal Away" became signals for action instead of mere escapist songs used in worship services.

When aggressive attempts were made to enforce the Fugitive Slave Act of 1850, disillusionment and despair increased the ranks of those free Negroes who wanted to go to either the Caribbean or Africa. The Dred Scott decision of 1857, also generated widespread feelings of disgust with the U.S. that caused many Negroes to decide it would be better to leave, though only a few did. One eminent Negro physician, Dr. Martin R. Delany, actually travelled to Nigeria to negotiate with a group of Yoruba chiefs for land and made arrangements for establishing a cotton growing scheme. He hoped to dump cotton on the world market at a low price and break the plantocracy.

While the black leadership was becoming polarized into those who counseled emigration and those who said, "Stay here," the white anti-slavery forces suffered a similar sharp rift in the North. Both the Negro and white anti-colonizationists were further polarized between those who were in favor of escalation of slave revolts and those who would only sanction non-violent means. The latter group, led predominantly by Quakers and including Unitarians, Methodists and Baptists, was shocked by one of the Southern responses to insurrections and anti-slavery propaganda. This was the activity of their fellow white Christians in the South who attempted to strengthen their control over the minds of the slaves by tightening up the supervision of their religious training, including attempts to prevent slaves from holding worship unless white people were present. Some Southern theologians were also circulating manuals with material for masters and mistresses to read to their slaves containing admonitions such as:

> "Almighty God hath been pleased to make you slaves here, and to give you nothing but labour and poverty in this world, which you are obliged to submit to, as it is his will that it should be so. Your bodies, you know, are not your own; they are at the disposal of those you belong to. . . ."

> "When correction is given you, you either deserve it or you do not deserve it. But whether you deserve it or not, it is your duty, and almighty God requires, that you bear it patiently . . ."

A "Catechism to be Taught Orally to Those Who Cannot Read" informed slaves that "to disobey your master is to yield to the temptation of the devil." All of this gave Christianity a bad name, and Walker rubbed the salt in the wounds, referring sarcastically to *"Christian* America" and to "the perverters" of the teachings of Christianity.

As Cotton gradually became King in the South after 1793, the humanitarians and religious sectarians had been thrown on the defensive by Southern "scholars" who were arguing that black skin was "the sign of the curse placed on Cain and his descendants" because he killed his brother Abel. The myth was already embedded in the mass culture of the nation as early as the time when Phyllis Wheatley who lived in Massachusetts pleaded with her fellow Christians:

> "Remember Christians, Negroes black as Cain
> May be refined, and join the angelic train."

The keystone of the theological argument, however, rested upon the curse that Noah was said to have placed upon the sons of Ham, dooming them to be hewers of wood and drawers of water to the sons of Shem and Japheth. Illiterate Negro preachers tried to

counter-attack by insisting that Noah was drunk when he pronounc-
ed the curse and therefore it was invalid. The white anti-slavery
ministers either took the position that the coming of Christ wiped
out the curse or just stubbornly reiterated the argument that God
is father and all men are brothers.

The Negro preachers, whether literate or illiterate, whether
they believed in insurrections or did not, whether they approved of
emigration or disapproved, felt impelled to counter-attack on a
more basic front. They were not only convinced that God would
eventually destroy the slave system in one way or another, but also
that the Bible did not support the position that black men were
cursed or inferior. Out of their offensive efforts a retrospective
myth of a glorious past and a prospective myth of eventual divine
deliverance took form, backed up by Biblical "proof-texts." As
soon as a semi-literate group emerged among the slaves, interpret-
ing the "open Bible" in the Protestant tradition, the possibilities
were present for developing a mythology to counter that used by
white Christians to degrade them.

Negro folk theologians were able to find the texts to counter
the derogatory scriptural interpretations. Black preachers may have
been advising the slaves to obey their masters and wait for the
Lord to show his hand, but they were also building group pride
and self-respect by naming their churches "African" and painting
a verbal picture of a glorious past. As soon as they became aware
that Egypt and Ethiopia were in Africa they were able to preach
and teach along these lines: God's own chosen people had to go
into Africa once, long ago, when the famine came, and Joseph became a great man in a black folks' kingdom. And then, when a
Pharaoh arose "who knew not Joseph" it was black men, wicked
ones but powerful ones, who put the Jews in slavery, forcing them
to make bricks without straw. Finally, when God raised up a de-
liverer among the Hebrew children he was educated by a kind
black princess, Pharaoh's daughter, and he married an Ethiopian
woman. When his own brother and sister "murmured against him"
because of the marriage God struck them down with leprosy until
they apologized. And how did they *know* these ancient people were
not *white* men? All of them were made out of the dust of the
earth and that's brown not white. And as for the Ethiopians, they
were the darkest of all, for did not the prophet Jeremiah ask, "Can

the Ethiopian change his skin? Can the leopard change his spots?"

The preachers talked about how the light browns sometimes looked down on the darker ones even in those biblical days, for the great King Solomon's black woman who loved him—and who got him—had to sing at those jealous women, "I am black but[1] comely, oh ye daughters of Jerusalem." And black women sometimes got "the dirty end of the stick" just like it happened on the plantation. When Father Abraham had a baby, Ishmael, by the bondservant, his wife, Sarah, made him put both the mother and the child out. That's why we call ourselves "Aunt Hagar's children."

But nothing could keep the black man down. Ethiopia was right there in the Bible alongside Egypt and Babylon and Assyria with her chariots and her mighty men of war. And when the wicked men threw the prophet of God, Jeremiah, into a dungeon, it was one of the "highups" at King Zedekiah's court, Ebed-Melech, the Ethiopian eunuch, who took him out and hid him.

There were New Testament passages too, to provide them with texts and stories for their sermons. Did not Joseph take Mary and the infant Jesus into Africa so the prophecy could be fulfilled, "Out of Egypt have I called my son?" And was it not an African, Simon of Cyrene, who picked up the cross and carried it when Jesus stumbled? Ethiopia was still a great kingdom in those latter days, because the Apostle Philip met the treasurer of Queen Candace riding home from Jerusalem in a chariot, converted him, and baptized him. We were not always white men's slaves and *our* time will come again, for the Bible says, "Princes shall come out of Egypt and Ethiopia shall soon stretch forth her hand unto God." Walker cited the prophecy in his *Appeal*.

This myth was a comforting morale builder and steeled those black people who believed it against those who tried to "rob them of their past." But it left unanswered a question, "Why was this ancient glory lost?" Insofar as they were believers in the Judaeo-Christian religion, they saw the same answer for themselves as for the Jews: "When a people forgets God and sins He'll bring them down! When they turn back to God again they'll be redeemed."

---

[1] Many of the more modern translations indicate that the original language really meant "black *and* comely."

One educated minister preaching in the early 1800s sounded the call to repentance, "Oh ye sons of Ethiopia, awake unto righteousness, for Jesus saith, 'Come unto me.' . . . Upon the wicked he shall rain fire and brimstone."

This Biblical myth is the core of a thought-style that might be called "Ethiopianism," and which became more complex and secularized as it developed during the 19th and 20th centuries. It emerged as a counter-myth to that of Southern white Christians (and many Northern ones). It functioned on a fantasy level giving feelings of worth and self-esteem to the individual, but also as a sanction for varied types of group action. It generated concern for the "redemption" of black men in the Motherland as well as the Diaspora so that the ancient state of power and prestige could be restored. It was the duty of black men who were "saved" to try to "convert" and "save" others—to preach the Gospel to their brothers wherever they might be, to enlighten them, to "civilize" them, to lift them from "their fallen state," to "redeem" them. Black Christians began at home working on the "sinners" in their midst. When their masters took them to the Caribbean they extended their evangelizing activity there. White Baptists had initiated some activity among the slaves in Jamaica by the middle of the 18th century, but the work did not begin to grow until a slave from America was brought there by his master after the Revolutionary War and so aroused his fellows that a distinctive Jamaican variety of the Baptist faith took root. As early as 1787 the first black American left for Africa to preach to his kinsmen there. Eventually, a Negro missionary movement gathered strength.

It was also not difficult for some black Christians to give an Ethiopianist twist to the white men's doctrine of Providential Design and to thus find a *modus vivendi* for co-operating with the colonization societies. One of the first Negro missionaries to Liberia, Daniel Coker, son of a Negro man and an English mother, taught to read and write by the son of his master. and who ran away to New York where he earned enough money to purchase his freedom, later opened an "African School" in Baltimore. Upon becoming a preacher he helped Richard Allen to organize the African Methodist Episcopal Church in 1816 and was elected its first bishop. Historian Hollis Lynch states that ". . . he declined the honor in order to go to Africa to help in laying of the foundation for a strong Negro nation." After a harrowing sea voyage to Africa under the auspices of the American Colonization Society he wrote in his journal, "O God! Why were we spared? Surely because this expedition is in the care of God—My soul travails that we may be faithful. And should God spare us to arrive in Africa that we may be useful." Lott Cary, a well-to-do Baptist minister in Richmond, Virginia, left for Liberia in 1815, with his family, declaring that "I am an African and in this country, however meritorious my conduct and respectably my character, I cannot receive the credit due either. I wish to go to a country where I shall be estimated by my merits not by my complexion." Although he went to Liberia under the colonization society, the American black Baptists eventually founded a missionary convention that bears his name. Another American Negro, Alexander Crummell, took a degree at Cambridge in England in 1853, and emigrated to Liberia. In a sermon delivered in Monrovia 40 years after the establishment of the republic, he gave eloquent expression to the Doctrine of Providential Design, referring to:

"the forced and cruel migration of our race from this continent, and the wondrous providence of God, by which the sons of Africa by hundreds and by thousands, trained, civilized, and enlightened, are coming hither again, bringing large gifts, for Christ and his Church, and their heathen kin."

He envisioned black history rising to a climax: "The day of preparation for our race is well nigh ended; the day of duty and responsibility on our part, to suffering, benighted, Africa, is at hand. In much sorrow, pain, and deepest anguish, God has been preparing the race, in foreign lands, for a great work of grace on this continent. The hand of God is on the black man in all the lands of his sojourn for the good of Africa." Crummell was not the only American Negro preacher who felt this way during the post-Civil War period. Bishop B. W. Arnett of the church founded by anti-colonizationist, Richard Allen, organized a company for trading with Africa in 1876, and favored the selective emigration of Negroes with some capital in order to help ". . . build up a New Christian Nationality in the Fatherland . . . that would cause Negroes everywhere to be respected."

51

By 1880, Alexander Crummell, disillusioned with the way in which the emigrants from America were conducting the affairs of Liberia, had returned home. Although Crummell returned to the United States there were other black ministers who remained ardent emigrationists. In fact, increasing discrimination against the Negro during the 1890's gave new impetus to Back-to-Africa movements and in 1901, Bishop Henry M. Turner of the A.M.E. Church wrote, in *Voice of the People:*

"The Negro Race has as much chance in the United States . . . of being a man . . . as a frog has in a snake den. . . . Emigrate and gradually return to the land of our ancestors. . . . The Negro was brought here in the providence of God to learn obedience, to work, to sing, to pray, to preach, acquire education, deal with mathematical abstractions and imbibe the principles of civilization as a whole, and then to return to Africa, the land of his fathers, and bring her his millions. . . ."

To give effect to these ideas he organized the Colored Emigration and Commercial Association which had a large following in some areas of the rural South, but sent no exiles home. The historian August Meier reminds us that "The persistence of emigrationist sentiment and the later mass appeal of the Garvey Movement suggests that perhaps the desire for colonization was more widespread among the masses than is generally believed. . . ."

The mainstream of sentiment within the Negro church, however, was not emigrationist, but it was always concerned with Africa. The concern found institutional expression through the mission boards of the Negro denominations which, in addition to their programs of evangelization, attempted to implement Bishop Arnett's dream of fostering trade with Africans, brought Africans to the United States for an education, and injected strong Ethiopianist elements into the doctrine of Providential Design. Negro missionaries, like their white counterparts, believed that Africa must be regenerated through the Gospel. The report of the Ecumenical Missionary Conference meeting in New York in 1900 contained a section on "A Work for American Negroes" with both white and Negro delegates stating that they thought black Americans had a special role. One Negro Baptist preacher castigated white missionaries for hampering the spread of the Gospel by importing race prejudice into Africa, citing this as one of the reasons why more Negro missionaries were desirable, but revealed his own *cultural* prejudices by his remarks about the "backwardness" of the Zulu people. He was expressing the general view of educated American Negroes, as revealed in the Indianapolis *Freeman*, a Negro newspaper, that had called for American intervention in the Congo in 1885, with the use of Negro settlers, for since "Africa is our Fatherland . . . we must prepare to enter upon the elevation of Africa with other races . . . civilizing our brethren . . . as well as Christianizing it."

The belief that Africa had a glorious past and that the people of the Diaspora were destined to help "redeem" it and "regenerate it" lent powerful impetus to the missionary movement of the Negro Methodist and Baptist churches and to Back-to-Africa movements that arose from time to time. The people involved believed that they were helping to speed the day when "Princes shall come out of Egypt and Ethiopia shall soon stretch forth her hand unto God." But this combination of Ethiopianism with the doctrine of Providential Design also stereotyped Africa as "heathen," "dark," and "benighted." While there was a tendency for black missionaries to differ from whites by trying to use the mission movement to stimulate commercial relations between Africans and American Negroes, and, occasionally, a black missionary put up a defense for some aspects of African culture, in general Negro missionaries were as censorious of African customs as white missionaries were. This troubled some of the more sensitive black secular intellectuals, but among preacher-scholars there was little sensitivity of this sort.

But of the theologically trained emigrants to Africa, one was very different from his fellows. He did not return to the land of the Diaspora, but, "playing for keeps," he not only achieved the international renown that Crummell never attained, but also transformed the doctrine of Providential Design and the myth of Ethiopianism into something of greater significance for the black world.

Edward Wilmot Blyden:
Intellectual Ethiopianist

Ethiopianism might have remained merely an escapist myth-system based upon Biblical proof-texts and confined to the circle of Negro church people had not a brilliant black scholar appeared on the scene in the 1870's and 1880's whose depth of learning and sound scholarship remolded it into an intellectually respectable "thought-style." He was a protege of the American Colonization Society but was also a man with a mind of his own who did not hesitate to use it. He became the first of a long line of Caribbean intellectuals who, while living in the United States, Europe, or West Africa contributed toward the development of ideology "situationally congruous," as Karl Mannheim would phrase it, with the status of black men in a world dominated by White Power. A perceptive biography of the man has been written by a fellow West Indian, Hollis Lynch's *Edward Wilmot Blyden: Pan Negro Patriot,* and another by the granddaughter of an American who befriended Blyden. A book published by him in 1887, *Christianity, Islam and the Negro Race,* has recently been reprinted with a valuable interpretative introduction by a British historian with insight, Christopher Fyfe, who reminds us that Blyden ". . . gave American Negroes a new vision of themselves in relation to their ancestral home" and that "Africans, too, were given a new vision of themselves as part of a wider identity than they had hitherto perceived." Blyden went out of vogue because of the secularization of ideologies and utopias during the early 20th Century, and because the kind of biological determinism that bolstered his theories about the distinctive traits of black men, and that interpreted the dynamics of history in terms of race, became intellectually disreputable between the two world wars. However, concepts of "Race pride," and "Race solidarity" articulated to neo-Marxian world views and without the biological baggage—*negritude,* Pan-Africanism, Pan-

Negroism, Black Power—have assumed political importance. Fyfe points out a significant contemporary fact, that all of Blyden is not "dated," and that "At last he has come into his own, and can be generally appreciated as the seminal, prescient philosopher that only a few years ago only a few recognized. No wonder statesmen and scholars turn to him for inspiration."

This "Pan-Negro Patriot" was born in the Danish West Indies of a free Negro family, and he claimed to be of "pure" Negro parentage of West African Ibo ethnic origin. His mother was a school teacher, his father a tailor. The family attended a Dutch Reformed Church with a racially mixed congregation, and young Blyden spent a great deal of time with Jewish neighbors from whom he acquired an interest in Hebrew history and in the adjustments of people in The Diaspora. At the age of 10 he went with his family to Venezuela, and while there, discovered that he had an unusual aptitude for learning languages. He attended the local St. Thomas schools before and after the Venezuela visit, and a white Presbyterian clergyman from the United States became his mentor and persuaded him to select the ministry as a career although he was apprenticed to a tailor. When Blyden was 18, he was taken to the United States and an attempt was made to enroll him at Rutgers. Refused there because of his color, he was then rebuffed by two other seminaries. He also had the harrowing experience of watching fugitive slaves being seized in Northern cities. He became resentful, fearful, and furious, and did not want to stay in the United States. Liberia had become an independent nation just two years before Blyden arrived in the United States, and the American Colonization Society was trying to recruit intelligent and ambitious settlers in order to prove that black men could handle their own affairs. The young West Indian was offered an opportunity to emigrate to Liberia, and Lynch states that "The idea of helping to build a great Negro nation in Africa appealed tremendously to the race-pride and imagination of Blyden. He unquestioningly accepted the current view that Africa was the 'dark continent' and that a new and progressive civilization would be created through the influence of westernized Negroes." He was converted to the doctrine of Providential Design. Twenty-seven years later, he was still expressing a conviction that "the deportation of the Negro to the New World was as much decreed by an all-wise Providence, as the expatriation of the Pilgrims from Europe . . . no indignation at the iniquities of unparalleled oppression in the house of bondage can prevent us from recognizing the hand of an over-ruling Providence in the deportation of Africans to the Western world, or interfere with our sense of the incalculable profit—the measureless gains—which, in spite of man's perversity, cruelty and greed, must accrue to Africa and the Negro race from the long and weary exile."

Blyden sailed for Africa eight months after he arrived in the United States and found employment as a clerk, pursuing part-time studies at a high school run by white American Presbyterian missionaries. The principal eventually persuaded Blyden's church back home in the Virgin Islands to pay his fees so he could attend full-time. He did well in the prescribed studies but "devoted most of his spare time to a study of Hebrew . . . so that he could read passages in the Bible purporting to relate to the Negro," even writing to a distinguished Jewish American scholar for a Hebrew grammar and commentaries on Genesis and Exodus. He began his intellectual journey with the same curiosity about Biblical references that led the illiterate folk preachers to elaborate the Ethiopian myth.

Within seven years Blyden was principal of the high school and had become an ordained minister as well. He then wrote the Presbyterian Board of Foreign Missions requesting a scholarship for two years of advanced study in the United States. His request was ignored. Blyden decided to secure a higher education "on his own," by wide and systematic reading of books, magazines, and newspapers and regular correspondence with learned men and women. Gladstone, the British Chancellor of the Exchequer, a classical scholar, encouraged him to continue his study of the Greek and Roman languages and literature, and sent him a small library."

Blyden's first use of his newly acquired classical knowledge for "racial vindication" seems to have been in a letter to the journal of the American Colonization Society answering a charge that Negroes were inferior to white men. He also referred to Africa as "the land of Cyprian and Tertullian, ancient fathers in the Christian Church; of Hannibal and Henry Diaz, renowned generals." Blyden was marshalling other data to support the Ethiopian myth than that found in the Bible.

Blyden eventually became a distinguished Liberian public official, representing that country twice at the Court of St. James, and was, for a while, the head of Liberia College. He took an active part in African exploration and travelled widely in Europe and America, but he also wrote continuously and gave addresses frequently, becoming ". . . easily the most learned and articulate champion of Africa and the Negro race in his own time." He never became a completely secular intellectual, however, but remained in the tradition of eminent and learned "divines" who still dominated much of the intellectual life of Europe and America. In 1857, at the age of 25, Blyden published his first solid work, *A Vindication of the Negro Race,* in which "He went to the extent of carefully examining the original Hebrew of verses 25, 26, and 27 of Chapter Nine of the Book of Genesis which were commonly cited to prove that Negroes—the offspring of Ham—were under a divine curse and that their enslavement was preordained." But Blyden first won favorable comment among scholars with an article in the *Methodist Quarterly Review,* twelve years later, in 1869, with an article on "The Negro in Ancient History." The article was based upon long and careful preparation, including a visit to Egypt, where, when he saw the Pyramids, he reported that "feelings came over me far different from those I ever felt when looking at the mighty works of European genius. I felt I had a peculiar heritage in the Great Pyramid built . . . by the enterprising sons of Ham, from which I was descended." He also wrote Gladstone for suggestions as to "sources of information on the Ancient Ethiopians." The data used in this article appeared in varying contexts for the rest of Blyden's life, and constitute the expansion of the Ethiopianist myth of the semi-literate American Negro ministers into an integrated thought-style providing a rationale for the missionary movement of black churches, the emigration movement to Africa, independent and separatist African churches, and various expressions of black nationalism.

Blyden's recasting of Ethiopianism begins with the reporting of a fact, that "In the earliest traditions of nearly all the more civilized nations of antiquity, the name of this distant people (*i.e.,* the Ethiopians) is found. The annals of the Egyptian priests were full of them; the nations of inner Asia, on the Euphrates and Tigris. . . . When the Greeks scarcely knew Italy and Sicily by

name, the Ethiopians were celebrated in verses of their poets as
. . .'The most just of men,' 'the favourites of the gods.' " For those
unfamiliar with the classical literature and who might think that
the references were to white North Africans and eastern Africans,
Blyden leaned heavily on Homer's reference to Eurybates in the
Iliad:

> A reverend herald in his train I knew,
> Of visage solemn, sad, but sable hue.
> Short wooly curls o'erfleeced his bending head
> O'er which a promontory shoulder spread;
> Eurybates, in whose large soul alone,
> Ulysses viewed an image of his own.

Herodotus spoke of two divisions of Ethiopians who differed only
from each other in language and hair, that of the "eastern Ethiopians being straight," that of the western Ethiopians being "more
curly than that of any other people." Blyden argued that references
to the Egyptians as a Colchi colony proved them to be black.

Both Lucian and Homer were cited to bolster the point that
the ancients thought of the Ethiopians as having superior virtues,
of being the people among whom the gods vacationed. As Homer
sang it,

> The Sire of gods and all the ethereal train
> On the warm limits of the farthest main
> Nor mix with mortals, nor disdain to grace
> The feasts of Ethiopia's blameless race . . .

Years later, a great mass leader, Marcus Garvey, embedded this
ancient myth in the anthem of his Universal Negro Improvement
Association. Blyden felt that the conclusion from his researches
showed that the ancients ". . . seemed to regard the fear and love
of God as the peculiar gift of the darker races, stating that in the
version of the Chaldean Genesis, as given by George Smith, the
following passage occurs, 'The word of the Lord will never fail in
the mouth of the dark races whom He has made.' " This belief in
the spiritual and moral superiority of black men also became a basic
dogma in later myth systems.

Blyden's strategy was to assemble evidence to support the argument that, having developed a high civilization in Egypt and Nubia, black men, "the Ethiopians," spread westward and southward so that by the time of Homer "they had not only occupied the northern provinces of Africa but had crossed the great desert, penetrated into the Soudan, and made their way to the West Coast." Thus, the ancient kingdoms of Ghana, Mali and Songhay, and the people carried off into the slave trade, were all descendants of the first civilizers—were Ethiopians. He stressed the point, too, that black people had been participants in the affairs of the classical Mediterranean civilizations, not only as slaves, but as soldiers in the Greek and Roman armies, and claimed, without convincing evidence, that Hannibal, the Carthaginian, was a Negro and was probably only one of several great black generals who had played a prominent role in the life of the ancient world.

In his later works, after he had studied Arabic, he singled out the prominent black men and women of the Islamic world for comment, beginning with Bilal, the friend of the prophet, and including a famous ruler in Bagdad. He began increasingly to assail the Christians for not only suppressing the great tradition, but also for deliberately concocting a myth of black inferiority to justify the trans-Atlantic slave trade. He saw his own scholarly work as contributing to the filling in of gaps and the setting of the record straight. Its effect on black people, he hoped would be to give them pride in their Race and to inspire them to help restore Africa to its former position of power and prestige.

Blyden's research into Biblical and classical sources might answer the question, "Who are we?" but did not answer the question, "Why our unhappy fate?" Blyden seems to have held to a philosophy of history that took the rise and fall of nations as a part of the order of nature and blended and intertwined it with theories of economic and geographic determinism. However, he never accepted the proposition that all black men "fell" or that the fate of the present generation was the result of the sins of the former—lack of good judgment or lack of power, yes; but divine punishment for sin, no. Yet, he did accept the doctrine of Providential Design, in his early years, almost as the white Christians taught it; although in later years, he explicitly rejected this aspect of it. Lynch, commenting upon this matter states,

"... it is clear what his philosophy of history was: the inscrutable working of Divine Providence for the ultimate good of the Negro Race. Such a view stemmed partly from his deeply religious nature and was partly a convenient rationale for the unhappy lot of his race." The function of this belief was, that of "... being able, theoretically at least, to salve the suffering and humiliation of the race in the past and in the present, while holding out to it the promise of a bright future." It was a useful retrospective and prospective myth when combined with Ethiopianism.

But Lynch feels that, though "... theocratic determinism—no more than an act of Faith—has its advantages, it led to contradictions in Blyden's whole scheme of thought and caused him to maintain ridiculous positions. He had, for instance, consistently argued that it was part of the Providential Design that Negroes should be taken to the New World so they could acquire Christianity and other elements of Western culture and civilization with the ultimate destiny of returning to christianize Africa." Thus, "Blyden in effect gave divine sanction to the slave trade, absolved those who had taken part in it, and nullified his argument that Christianity had stunted the 'growth of manhood' among New World Negroes."

That Blyden was aware of being open to this type of criticism is apparent in an article he wrote in the 1880's where, after affirming his belief in Providential Design, he went on to apportion blame rather than to absolve all:

"When we say that Providence decreed the means of Africa's enlightment, we do not say that He decreed the wickedness of the instruments. . . . It was not the first time that wicked hands were suffered to execute a Divine purpose. . . ."

The "wicked" men were involved in what he called "... the slave trade, with all its unspeakable enormities." As Blyden matured, reshaping his intellectual formulations in the light of his experience and historic events, he was able, after the abolition of slavery in the United States, to say in an address to the American Colonization Society in 1880 on "Ethiopia Stretching Out Her Hands Unto God, or Africa's Service to the World," that abolition was in the "Design": "The ways of God are mysterious. We must walk by faith and not by sight. We hear His voice saying 'This is the way; walk ye in it.' In the raising of this Society *and the doing away with slavery* we can see almost visibly the hand of God displayed."

The doctrine of Providential Design was elaborated by both black and white Christians, sharing as they did a common theology, but since only white people had the economic resources to send missionaries and Negro emigrants to Africa, Negroes were allocated their role in the implementation of the "Design" by white men, who even developed a sub-dogma, that God had provided a type of man resistant to fevers and the African sun, who if sent to Africa could survive better than the white man. Blyden accepted this dogma and even sought to keep it alive, but to serve other ends —to discourage white settlement in West Africa.

As early as 1855, the British Christians were training Negroes from the West Indies for work in the Rio Pongo mission. Blyden did not disapprove, for if white mission boards were to operate in the field he preferred that black men be the agents. But he was anxious for New World Negroes to mobilize their own resources so they could control the missionary movement. In a discussion of how necessary it was that ". . . for the spiritual war which is being carried into Africa, the church must utilize the African," he remarked:

"The African Methodist Episcopal Church in the United States (soon to be joined by the African Methodist Episcopal Zion Church, and similar organizations), in machinery and appliances, and in physical adaptation, leads the way. The Negro Baptists of the South are already in the field. There are Negro Presbyterians and Negro Episcopalians. These will all be utilized when a few more years, and a little more experience, have satisfactorily demonstrated to the American Church the utter impracticability of the present methods. 'Arm the Negroes! Arm the Negroes! will ring again through the American nation. Arm the Negroes in the name of Christ. If Africa is to be conquered for Christ.'"

Although Blyden encouraged the missionary movement of the black churches, and they developed with an Ethiopanist orientation suffusing their concept of Providential Design, he did not play any crucial role in the process. Their movement sprouted from the

61

seed-bed of folk-Ethiopianism. His great intellectual contribution was to develop a line of thought that ultimately was turned back in criticism of Negro missionaries as well as white ones. His great contribution was toward the development of African "cultural nationalism." The dominant view among missionaries, white and black, at the time was that African cultures were "degenerated" and needed "regeneration." Negroes intergrated this idea into their Ethiopianism of the Biblical variety. Blyden repudiated this view as his own thinking developed. Lynch notes that:

> "From early in his writings Blyden assumed the role of defender of African culture . . . he warned Europeans that if they were to be useful in Africa they would have to lay aside their arrogant assumption of the superiority of European culture, recognize that African culture was, on the whole, best suited to the circumstances of the African people, and carefully study African society, so as not to destroy any customs and institutions which were important and humane elements of African culture."

After the partition of Africa began in 1884, Blyden felt that the danger of the disintegration of African society was increased and wrote a great deal on this theme. His last and most ambitious piece of work, published only four years before his death was *African Life and Customs.* Many years were to elapse before mission boards would be sympathetic to this point of view, and most African customs were as repugnant to the black "Christian conscience" as to the white.

From the 1880's onward, however, American Negro missionaries increasingly felt as did the Baptist missionary, C. C. Boone, who wrote, "So many have written and spoken concerning my people in Africa and have either attributed all of their ingenuity to the white man or discredited their capabilities altogether, that I am glad to be able to give a true testimony of what I really saw in the land of my fathers." He then proceeded to praise the Congo Africans for their skill in farming and for the orderliness of their domestic and public life. The mission movement in Africa was started by whites in 1787, and their boards dominated the scene, but the American Negro denominations eventually added a distinctive dimension of their own to the effort. They came to be feared as subversive throughout Africa partly because their very presence there presented an example of what Africans could be and do if they had a chance to secure an education. Sometimes their influence was more directly disturbing, as in the case of John Chilembwe, who, after studying at a Negro school in America (the Virginia Theological Seminary and College) returned home to found the Baptist Industrial Mission in Nyasaland and to carry out a program of trade in collaboration with the Negro Baptists in America. George Shepperson and Thomas Price in their fascinating work, *Independent African*, have told the tragic story of how he became involved in the uprising in his native land in 1915 and was hanged.

Hollis Lynch is correct in his conclusion that Blyden's writings, taken as whole, are "a curious blend of propaganda in scholarship, of the messianic, the mystical and metaphysical with the historical and sociological." One "mystical" and "metaphysical" aspect of Blyden's thought fed into the stream of belief in "black messianism" or "Negro messianism" that was growing up among both the religious and secular New World Negro leaders. In 1882, Blyden called Negroes "to remember that if they were despised and scorned, a far greater than themselves had had a similar experience . . . they have been chosen to tread in the footsteps of the first born of the creation suffering for the welfare of others. . . . All the advancement made to a better future by individuals or race, has been made through paths marked by suffering. This great law is written not only in the Bible, but upon all history." As Blyden saw it, this suffering would lead eventually to a renascent Africa, independent and sovereign. The suffering of the people of the Diaspora would redeem all black men.

Since Black Nationalism seemed unrealistic to the moderate black leaders as a goal for American Negroes, the concept as developed in the United States from Booker T. Washington to Martin Luther King, Jr. (with overtones even in Stokely Carmichael) was that their suffering would "save" America and the world. Benjamin Mays quoting Dr. Robert Russa Moton, Booker T. Washington's successor, in *The Negro's God*, selects the following passage to illustrate Moton's belief that "what the Negro has suffered in this country is a part of the plan of God":

"Thinking of the experiences through which my ancestors passed, along with thousands of other slaves, in their contact

with the white people of America, I have often felt that some-
how in spite of the hardships and oppressions which they suffered—that in the providence of God, the Negro . . . has come
through the ordeal with much to his credit. . . . And how shall
we account for it, except it be that in the providence of God
the black race in America, was thrust across the path of the onward marching white race to demonstrate, not only for America, but for the World, whether the principles of freedom are of
universal application, and ultimately to extend its blessings to
all mankind. . . . In the providence of God there has been
started on these shores the great experiment of all the ages—
Here in America the two races are charged, under God, with
the responsibility of showing the world how individuals as
well as races may differ most widely in color and inheritance
and at the same time make themselves helpful and even indi-
spensable to each others progress and prosperity."

In contrast to Booker T. Washington and his followers, W. E. B.
DuBois, Negro elder statesman and radical free-thinker, who became a Communist and emigrated to Ghana in his 90's, elaborated
a secularized version of "the suffering servant" as expressed through
"black messianism." He revealed his conviction in a long poem in
the 1960's that it was the destiny of Africans to show white men
how *real* socialism would operate. Those who had suffered most
had the most to teach their Marxist comrades.

What seem to be logical contradictions in Blyden's thought may
seem less contradictory if they are related to time and place, and
the degreee of his power or powerlessness at specific periods in his
life to attain goals he had set for himself. When American Negroes
turned out to be generally lukewarm about emigration, Blyden
shifted to a "remnant theory"—that only some of the Exiles were
destined to be Ingathered—or were even wanted. Later, he extended
the time span over which he felt even their return would take place.
Later, all of his earlier views about the special and almost messianic
role of New World Negroes were abandoned. With him Ethiopianism ceased to be either an escapist ideology for people in the
Diaspora or a spur to emigration, and became, rather, an ideology
sanctioning the development of Africa by Africans themselves—
not by New World Negroes. This point of view developed as he

became an integral part of West African political and intellectual activity.

Until the year 1871, Blyden lived and worked continuously in Liberia and was a firm believer in the possibility of building that nation into a first-class power if a constant stream of well selected immigrants flowed in regularly from the New World. This meant being careful not to kick out from under him the stool on which he stood, the American Colonization Society, that had the means to finance his own trips to America on recruiting missions as well as voyages of black emigrants to Africa. While he never compromised his espousal of Ethiopianism in dealing with them, he did speak much more to them of Providential Design in its orthodox variety than when he was among others.

After Blyden had won some degree of eminence and esteem in Africa, while visiting the United States on a speaking tour sponsored by the American Colonization Society, he reminded those who had sent him to Africa as a young man that "The descendants of the Africans in this country have never needed the stimulus of any organization of white men to direct their attention to the land of their fathers." (He was referring of course to people like Paul Cuffee and the 18th Century Massachusetts enslaved petitioners.) To Blyden, "The Colonization Society was only the instrument of opening a field for the energies of the Africans who desired to go and avail themselves of the opportunities offered there." Later, he abandoned the Doctrine of Providential Design completely.

As the years passed and Blyden had a number of personal difficulties with Liberian officials, he came to blame the "failure" of Liberia on the fact that it had attracted too many mulatto immigrants who did not have pride of race ("blood" theories were in vogue at the time), and he came to express virtual hatred of mulattoes and to discourage them from coming to Liberia. After the Civil War, as smaller and smaller numbers of Negroes in the U.S. displayed any interest in emigrating, he blamed this upon a mulatto leadership in America that not only despised Africa, but also wanted to keep black Afro-Americans in the United States where they could exploit them despite the fact that full equality for the masses would never come.

Eventually Blyden made Sierra Leone the base of his operations rather than Liberia, and received financial assistance from wealthy

Africans, making him less dependent upon white Americans or America-Liberians. In this phase of his life one notes a shift away from expressions of the doctrine of Providential Design in its original form, coupled with a tendency to make severe criticisms of or- from expressions of the doctrine of Providential Design in its original form, coupled with a tendency to make severe criticism of organized Christianity and to contrast it unfavorably with Islam. His interest in Islam had begun early and now increased. In 1887, a group of Blyden's Sierra Leone African admirers encouraged him to publish fifteen of his articles and essays under the title, *Christianity, Islam and the Negro Race.* One of these was an article he had written in 1871 for the *Methodist Quarterly Review* on "Mohammendanism in West Africa." It summarized his thinking of a decade after contact with Muslims in the interior of West Africa and the study of Islamic writings, he having learned Arabic. He lauded the Muslims for their ban on alcoholic drinks, their devotion to learning, and the stimulus they gave to artisan crafts and trade. Four years later, after two expeditions into the interior of Sierra Leone, he wrote "Mohammedanism and the Negro Race." This was, in essence, a commentary on a series of lectures by a British scholar who was trying to correct derogatory stereotypes about Muslims, a very approving commentary. A new note is added to his former article in his stress on the point that "There are numerous Negro communities and states in Africa which are self-reliant, productive, independent" and that most of these were Islamic, the culture being essentially African however. He argued that from the beginning, Islam had been without race prejudice and Africans had held high positions, documenting this from his study of a French translation of Ibn Khallikan's *Biographies.* He assailed Christianity for having imposed inequalities upon black people and felt that the absence of pictorial representation in Islamic societies had saved black people from having great and holy people always depicted to them as white. He even defended *jihads,* or holy wars, on the grounds that these involved Africans—and not outside conquerors —trying to lift the cultural level of other Africans!

Two articles were written especially for the volume and their significance lies in the fact that they were written after the "partition" began: "Islam and Race Distinctions" and "The Mohammedans of Nigritia." He felt that, on balance, Muslim conquest had

66

been more beneficial to Africans than European imperialism because it ". . . left the native master of himself and of his home" and was not racist. Blyden gradually moved from a position of asking tolerance for Moslems to visualizing them as preparing pagan peoples for the acceptance of Christianity as a religion for Africans. He shocked many of his former supporters, and there were those who accused him of favoring Islam because it allowed polygamy, Blyden having taken on a "second wife," a darker, younger American Negro woman. But such an explanation was, of course, too simple. He was convinced that Islam met African needs better than Christianity. On the intellectual level, praise of Islam offered a solution to the problem of "degenerationism." He was able to argue that centuries before the Europeans came there were some Africans who had stable *non-pagan* cultures in Northern and Western Africa, carrying on the civilizing work that African Christians and Jews in East Africa had begun early in the Christian era. As for the pagans, they were simply people like the European barbarians who had not been elevated by civilizing influences traceable back to Egypt. Then, on contact with Islam their cultures flourished. The enthusiasm for Islam tended to cut him off from black Christians in the New World, for they, like the whites, defined Mohammedans as heathens to be converted, not people to be admired. Blyden remained a Christian but was suspected of being a Muslim at heart. (This turning toward Islam for identification has cropped up among Negroes of the Diaspora in more recent times.)

As Blyden's disillusionment with Negro Americans and with Liberia increased, his faith in African initiative grew. He visualized the emergence of a great West African nation cutting across all artificially imposed political boundaries. However, to achieve this goal powerful allies were needed, not a small colonization society in the United States. He gradually loosened his bonds with this group who believed that Providential Design allotted a crucial place to New World Negroes. Blyden had fled to Sierra Leone in 1871 during a political crisis in Liberia and remained there for three years. He became convinced that Liberia and Sierra Leone should be merged to form a single state, sovereign, but under British guidance in the early stages, feeling that a vigorous intellectual community had been allowed to grow up in Sierra Leone under British rule that could energize the larger nation. For the next 13 years he used his influence toward this end, even when he was Liberia's ambassador to England in 1877.

In an article published in 1878, "Africa and Africans," he counseled close co-operation between Africans and friendly European powers, suggesting that "Providence used men and nations for higher purposes than they themselves conceived." By now he was thinking of a great "West African community" that would evolve gradually into a "West African nation." He felt that the climate and the diseases were a providentially-provided protection against permanent white settlement. In 1884, at the Congress of Berlin, the partition of all of Africa began. Blyden saw God's hand in this, too, but Africans must be astute and active participants in the process. He gave first priority to the strengthening of the Muslim communities and states throughout West Africa. By 1886 he was diligently improving his Arabic and expanding his first-hand contact with Muslim leaders. Hostile at first to French penetration into West Africa because he considered them too assimilationist and because they were destroying Muslim states, he later came to hold them up as a model to the British for their policy of according status and respect to traditional African rulers.

As British power became consolidated in the Gold Coast and Nigeria, Blyden began to try to convince his British friends that the populous and prosperous Nigerian colony and protectorates could be the core of a prosperous, friendly, West African trade area. In 1896, his advocacy bore fruit and he was appointed Agent for Native Affairs in Lagos, Nigeria. Cultural nationalism, not political nationalism, was his prescription for the period and he tried to forge links between intellectuals in Sierra Leone, the Gold Coast, Liberia, and Nigeria, and to agitate for a West African university. He became a proponent of indirect rule and may have had some influence upon its eventual adoption as British policy. In 1901, he was appointed Director of Mohammedan Education in Sierra Leone. The British co-operated with him in his efforts to draw Muslims into the administration of their territories, they dreaming of permanent indirect rule and he of some eventual shaking off of British tutelage and the emergence of a great black nation. But of this far off event he spoke little.

So convinced was Blyden that European imperialism was a necessary step in preparing Africans for the task of modern self government that he praised German colonial administration, and would not even criticize King Leopold for permitting atrocities in the Congo! He had stated his view, in 1878, of imperialists in an article on "African and Africans," that "retribution for their misdeeds will come from God." In 1900, Blyden was 68 years old. The Liberians considered him a "sell-out" to the British; younger African intellectuals pointed out the contradiction in his glorifying African traditionalism (and what many considered "paganism") while he himself competed for prestige in world literary circles and was conventionally British in tastes and habits (except for the "mistress" and his bias toward Islam); Christians, white and black, disapproved of his defense of "heathen customs" and Mohammedanism. His older, wealthy, African patrons were dead and he was ailing. He wrote to an influential British friend in 1910:

"I am now in feeble health and living from hand to mouth. The Sierra Leonans, among whom I have hitherto received sympathy and support, are now indifferent because I cannot encourage them in their misguided course [a demand for greater immediate self-government]. . . . The natives now avoid me as the Liberians do, because I am pointing out the way of life and prosperity for them. . . . My expenses of fifteen weeks in the hospital have left me in debts, and the Liberians, men whom I have taught and in other ways assisted, seem to have no idea of restoring my pension. History repeats itself; the people kill the prophets: Cicero, Demosthenes, Socrates, [no Biblical prophets mentioned] must go if the unprincipled demagogues so will."

The Governors in Sierra Leone, Nigeria and the Gold Coast granted him a pension of $375 a year. He died on February 7, 1912.

Lynch, in assessing Blyden's significance, states that "More than any other Negro in the nineteenth century, Blyden's writing and scholarship have won him widespread recognition and respect in the English-speaking literary world as well as acclaim in the Muslim world." Blyden prized this recognition and acclaim, but what he probably prized even more was the tribute paid to him by West Africa's most distinguished native-born man of letters, who was later to found the Congress of British West Africa, J. E. Casely-Hayford of the Gold Coast, who in his book *Ethiopia Unbound*, published the year before Blyden died, called him, in the Afro-Christian idiom, ". . . a god descended upon earth to teach Ethiopians anew the way of life . . . a John the Baptist among his brethren, preaching rational and national Salvation. . . . 'What shall it profit a race if it shall gain the whole world and lose its soul?'"

The American Negro leaders who were Blyden's contemporaries respected him as a scholar and accorded him considerable deference and honor whenever he visited the United States. However, they saw little in his political philosophy—in each successive stage of its development—other than his emphasis upon "race pride." After his death, Blyden's name faded out of the consciousness of American Negro scholars, race leaders, preachers, and so he did not become one of the heroes in the Negro history pantheon. In West Africa, on the other hand, despite his lack of popularity in some African circles, Blyden's name remained a household word among educated Africans. In 1913, a large bust was erected in his honor in Freetown, Sierra Leone, by his British admirers, while his African friends and admirers placed a headstone over his grave with inscriptions in gold. Stained glass windows memorialized him in the largest meeting hall in Lagos, Nigeria, along with a photograph bearing the caption, "Greatest Defender of the Negro Race."

The inheritors of J. Casely-Hayford's mantle in the Congress of British West Africa clung to Blyden as a symbol of their prime values—a cultural resurgence and West African political union. Herbert Macaulay, who founded the National Council of Nigeria and the Cameroons, passed on the Blyden "legend" to his successor, Dr. Nnamdi Azikiwe, the Nigerian nationalist leader and newspaper publisher, who, in a foreword to a biography of Blyden in 1967, wrote, "Dr. Blyden rightly has been referred to as a father of African nationalism." At least two primary schools have been named for Blyden in Nigeria and a grandson, Edward Blyden III, was appointed to the political science department at the University of Nigeria with appropriate publicity.

Contemporary West African nationalists have used Blyden in their own process of myth-making and symbol-building as an example of early "black achievement," ignoring his pro-British conservative stance. They stress his role in the development of "race pride" and cultural nationalism. New World Negro scholars are rediscovering his pioneer role as a "Pan-Negro Patriot."

Ethiopianism
and Religious-Political Movements

Blyden's Ethiopianism was utilized only incidentally as a sanction for the Christian missionary movement. He utilized it primarily as a sanction for New World emigration to Africa. Near the end of his life, Blyden abandoned his interest both in emigration from the New World and in the missionary movement. The logical end of Ethiopianist thinking is the position that Africans, themselves, are thoroughly competent to chart their own course of development and to manage their own affairs. When shorn of Christian beliefs about "degeneration" and "redemption" through conversion to Christ, Ethiopianist thinking leads to a belief that the forces are latent within Africa itself to "redeem" it. Blyden came to believe that the most potent forces lay in the African variety of Islam, but that Africans could adapt Christianity to their needs just as they had with Islam. This would mean, however, the replacement of the missionary movement—especially where controlled by whites—with an autonomous African church. The history of Christianity in ancient North Africa and Ethiopia—and especially in Ethiopia—was cited as proof of African religious genuis. In 1890, he formed a close and enduring friendship with a Nigerian, Majola Agbebi, who was one of the main architects of the Independent Baptist Native Church, the forerunner of what eventually came to be called "separatist" and "independent" churches in Africa.

Hollis Lynch describes the Nigerian movement briefly: "Agbebi had continued to strive for an African Church free of foreign trappings; thus in 1898 he excluded the use of wine as a sacrament in the services of the Native Baptist Church, partly as a protest against the trade in liquor in West Africa. . . . In 1895, he persuaded a West Indian couple, the Rev. J. E. Ricketts and his wife, to join his church as 'Industrial Missionaries.' . . . In his missionary and educational work Agbebi refused to recognize the territorial

71

boundaries drawn by the European imperialist powers. . . . **He** pointed out to prospective converts that conversion to Christianity would not entail the disruption of the soical fabric by giving up such wholesome customs as polygamy . . . several chiefs became Christian converts and placed their sons and nominees under his instruction. Agbebi's drive and organizing ability can be estimated by the fact that by 1903 he had organized and become President of the Native Baptist Union of West Africa which included churches in Sierra Leone, Ghana (Gold Coast), Nigeria, and the Cameroons." Blyden encouraged him in his ambition to merge the Native Baptist Church with another group, the United Native African Church, to form the African Church of Lagos, and to eventually organize "a united West African Church." In commenting on a sermon by Agbebi he wrote to him: "No one can write on the religion of the African as an African can . . . and you have written thoughtfully and with dignity and impressiveness . . . 'Africa is struggling for a separate personality' and your discourse is one of the most striking evidences of this. The African has something—a great deal to say to the world . . . which it ought to hear." One of Blyden's favorite expressions, probably coined by him, was "The African Personality." Kwame Nkrumah revived it in the 20th century.

The West African separatist and independent church movement was "Ethiopianist" in spirit although it did not use the word. During the same period, however, a similar movement in South Africa explicitly designated itself as such. Here, a group of preachers, some of whom had studied at Negro schools in the U.S.A., expressed their dissatisfaction with white missionary controls by setting up their own congregations, some of which sought affiliation with the African Methodist Episcopal Church of the Negroes in America. The story has been told by Bengt Sundkler in *Bantu Prophets* and he divides the churches into two groups, the otherworldly non-political "zionist" sects that became affiliated with a white denomination in the U.S.A., and the "Ethiopianists," who took as their slogan, "Princes shall come out of Egypt and Ethiopia shall soon stretch forth her hand unto God." The government viewed the Ethiopian churches as subversive; the missions defined them as semi-pagan and blasphemous, except for the Church of England which tried to contain and channel the protest by wooing congregations back into its orbit as affiliates of "The Order of Ethiopia" sanctioned by the Anglican Church. The term "Ethiopianism" became embedded in the literature of journalists and scholars to apply to this particular movement, and it has been generalized and extended as a concept referring to a thought-style in this work.

The popularity of the term in the 1890's was enhanced by events actually occurring in Ethiopia. Black nationalists had clung to Liberia and Haiti as symbols of black sovereignty even when they disapproved of the internal politics in those countries or were embarrassed by their "lack of progress." Now, in the 1890's a new symbol of black nationalism pushed Liberia and Haiti into the background. While Blyden was using his quite considerable scholarship to prove that *all* black Africans were Ethiopians and therefore that any Biblical prophecies that referred to Ethiopia referred to black Africa as a whole and that her "redemption" was certain, the one spot left that bore the name, the inheritor of the ancient glory, stirred the whole black world. Most of the continent had been partitioned between 1884 and 1890 by England, France, Germany, Portugal and Belgium. Italy had secured a foothold on the Red Sea in what is now Eritrea and Somalia. In 1889, she had aided Menelik in establishing himself on the imperial throne of Ethiopia and the two countries signed a treaty of friendship. In 1891, Britain signed a treaty with Italy recognizing Ethiopia as being in that European country's "sphere of influence." With some encouragement from France, Menelik denounced the treaty as a trap. England then encouraged Italy to assert its authority and to declare a protectorate over Ethiopia. In 1895, Italy crossed the border and started advancing into the Ethiopian highlands. On March 1, 1896, Menelik and his forces struck back and shattered the Italian army at Adowa. For the first time in modern history an African nation had defeated a white nation. When the peace treaty was signed, Italy paid Ethiopia an indemnity of $2,000,000 and recognized the "absolute independence" of the ancient empire. Menelik became a hero throughout the black world. He was the harbinger of the "redemption of Africa" that would someday come to pass. Ethiopia replaced Haiti and Liberia as the master symbol of Black Power and Black Nationalism.

Between the end of the 19th Century and the outbreak of World War I in 1914, there was a gradual secularization of black leadership in the United States, the West Indies and Africa. As in-

73

creasing numbers of college graduates emerged who were not trained in theology, the "vindication of the Race" passed from the hands of those who believed in Providential Design and Biblically sanctioned "Ethiopianism" into the hands of professionally trained historians, anthropologists, and archaeologists. After 1900, Pan Africanism gradually became the dominant political myth of the black world—replacing the Ethiopianist pre-political myth. But Ethiopianism was by no means dead. It has persisted in its oldest and most theological form in the churches of the unsophisticated in the U.S.A. and South Africa. It became a basic subsidiary reinforcing myth for the great black nationalist mass movement of the 1920's, Marcus Garvey's Universal Negro Improvement Association (UNIA). By the mid 1920's Ethiopianist ideas were so deeply imbedded in the urban subcultures of the Afro-American urban communities, from the impact of the Negro church and the UNIA, that an apperceptive mass was present to which founders of cults and social movements could appeal. All of these cults provide meaningful schemes of living and answers to the identity quest for a small fraction of the black population in the United States. Their political significance as organized groups is minimal, but their influence on ghetto thinking has sometimes been significant.

Some of the cults are explicitly Ethiopianist. As early as 1919, a small group of "Abyssinians" were active in Chicago and were accused of fomenting violence in the Black Belt. The Italian attack on Ethiopia in the 1930's focussed attention upon two small groups that had been organized in the early Thirties, the *Ethiopian World Federation* and the *Ethiopian Peace Movement,* the latter of which had a strong Back-to-Africa emphasis.

Other cults are Islamic. In 1913, a North Carolina Negro, Timothy Drew, changed his name to Noble Drew Ali and founded a Moorish Science Temple in Newark, New Jersey, that soon had branches in Detroit, Harlem, Chicago, Pittsburgh, Philadelphia and a number of southern cities. The members called themselves "Moors" and wore red fezzes. Their belief was that "Christianity is for the European (paleface); Moslemism is for the Asiatic (olive-skinned)." All black people were "Asiatics." In the 1930's what eventually became the Black Muslim movement emerged, urging "so-called Negroes" to give up their slave names, to return to their true religion, Islam, and to separate themselves from the "blue eyed devils." This was preached as the way for the "tribe of Shebazz," the "Lost-Found Nation in the Wilderness of North America" to come together and to save themselves from the doom that Allah has prepared for their oppressors.

Not all of the American Negro cult founders have been oriented toward Ethiopia or have moved, as Blyden did, toward identification with Islam. Some have become Black Jews with a myth of their own origin as having been among the Falashas, the Black Jews of Ethiopia, who have resided there for centuries. The Commandment Keepers in New York are closest to Orthodox Judaism in belief. and ritual. Of three groups in Chicago, the oldest claims superiority over "fair-skinned" Jews who are believed to be descended from Aaron and Miriam whose skin never returned to its original brown color after they were struck with leprosy for their criticism when Moses married an Ethiopian woman. Of the most recently organized group of Black Jews in Chicago, over 200 emigrated to Liberia in 1967.

The cults in the United States have attracted very few members, but in Jamaica, the Ras Tafarians, who think of Haile Selassie as their God-King, have become an important part of the island subculture and have a political potential that gives some concern to the government. Out of their ranks have come a few artists and poets; and *New World*, a magazine of moderate left-wing intellectuals, published a poem in 1968 by one of them:

REPATRIATION POEM
by Ras Dizzy

O Clergymen of the Babylon Fort
What power have thee got?
Remove those blindfolds
Unlock those gates
Our King has called us home.

O Africa's Sons and Daughters,
I hear a fife playing.
The tune is ours but the music is slow
We might have known the Captain
But the ship is far at Sea.

75

Questions
for Discussion
and Further Research

1. In the first section of the essay (especially p. 16) Drake seems to accept the validity of the popular concept that a sharp line of distinction existed between house servants and those of our forefathers who worked in the fields during the time of slavery. He refers to a "totally different" way of life and a fierce determination among the house servants to protect their special privileges. Is there any evidence to support this as a valid generalization? For instance, how carefully have we examined the role of house servants in insurrectionary plots, apart from the well-publicized informers?

2. Beginning on p. 12, Drake calls attention to the differences between what he called an "African-American" culture which developed in the Caribbean and South America on the one hand, and the rise of an "Afro-American" culture in North America. He suggests that economic, demographic and acculturational factors account for this difference. What were some of these factors? Drake does not mention political factors. What was their nature and their role?

3. Drake claims that Frederick Douglass "never displayed any special interest in Africa. . . ." Is there documentation to support this generally held view? A serious investigation of Douglass' words and deeds on this subject would likely prove illuminating.

4. On p. 22, Drake suggests that African religion contained no categories which would allow it to speak to the anguished question of *"Why?"*—why were we allowed to experience the unspeakable horrors of the Diaspora? Similarly, some new world Africans have claimed that African religion and philosophy—with their great emphasis on tradition and orderly change—have no place for concepts of revolution. Are the imposed, oppressive experiences of the last 500 years so qualitatively different and distinctive from

76

the millenia-long pilgrimage on the mainland that they demand a new set of religious categories for African peoples? What are the possible sources of these new developments of religious life and thought?

5. It has been suggested that while he often breaks the barriers of sterile academic disciplines in this provocative essay, Brother Drake still approaches Black religion essentially as a cultural anthropologist. Therefore he misses some of the deepest non-rational significance of the charismatic, numinous experience which constantly explodes across the arena of black religion. What do you think of this comment? Are there any methodological tools which are more adequate for a study of Africanized religion? Can it ultimately be known without personal immersion in the experience?

6. In his discussion of Haiti and its powerful impact upon black (and white) consciousness here in the United States, Brother Drake contrasts the North American and Haitian situations. At one point he says: "The sobering fact had to be faced that what a black majority could do on the island of Haiti was quite different from what a black minority embedded in the heart of a large white nation could realistically hope for." Elsewhere, speaking of slave rebellions and their goals, he asked: ". . . what, indeed, was success? What were the goals other than vengeance?"

What responses are possible to those questions and assumptions? How, for instance, shall we understand adequately what the participants in rebellions hoped for? What modern relevance do the questions have?

7. Drake claims that "Richard Allen [was] convinced that forces were at work that would bring the end of slavery without violent insurrection." He goes on to cite the actions of Thomas Jefferson and George Washington, calling them "leaders in the movement for manumission or voluntary emancipation. . . ." The idea that such opinions were prevalent before the rise of the cotton industry is a popular one. However, recent scholarship suggests that belief in the imminent unviolent demise of slavery was not as widely held in the pre-cotton-gin United States as some have thought. See, for instance, Donald Robinson, *Slavery in the Structure of American Politics, 1765-1820.* (New York, 1971).

8. Drake refers in several places to the intentions of 19th Century Black Americans to set up extensive commercial ties between Africans in the homeland and in the Diaspora. Garvey was an obvious benefactor of this earlier thinking, but little research has been done on these roots of Garvey's thinking. It would be important to examine this history of commercial ties—actual and projected—to see how its proponents fitted into the larger concern for the redemption of Africa.

9. Brother Drake assumes at several points that black and white Christians of the 19th century shared "a common theology." Is this assumption justified? What, indeed, were the theological frameworks out of which black Christians operated, especially those who were held in slavery? Did they maintain the same world view, have the same doctrine of man, and sin and ethics and eschatology as whites? None of the relatively few studies of the antebellum Negro Church really ask these questions in detail. The answers (and the questions) are important for an understanding of the ground out of which we have sprung—and in which many of us currently stand.

10. Drake has opened an important area of research in the concept of Ethiopianism in Black America. Its presence in the thought of Africans in America needs careful examination, and the specific organizational manifestations which still exist—like the Ethiopian World Federation—should be more fully understood.

11. When "Ethiopianism" and Christian based concepts of "Providential Design" and "Black Messianism" are replaced by Marxist-based versions of Pan-Africanism and "secular" Black Messianism, we really have one set of religious myths (sometimes called world views) substituted for another. If the time ever comes when black people are no longer able to commit themselves to any overarching world views, and instead live in the polluted, secular cubicles called existence in white America, apart from gods, spirits and fathers, what will we tell our children when they ask us *WHY?* Or will the courage—and the concern—to ask that question have also passed in the post-myth period?

A Selected
Reading List of Books
Referred to by St. Clair Drake

Allen, Richard. *The Life Experiences and Gospel Labors of the Rt. Rev. Richard Allen.* New York: Abingdon Press, 1960.

Aptheker, Herbert. *American Negro Slave Revolts.* New York: International Publishers, 1963.

—————. *A Documentary History of the Negro in the United States.* Vol. I. New York: Citadel Press, 1968.

—————. *One Continual Cry—David Walker's Appeal to the Coloured Citizens of the World.* New York: Humanities Press, 1965.

Blyden, Edward W. *African Life and Customs.* London: African Publication Society, 1969.

—————. *Christianity, Islam and the Negro Race.* Edinburgh: Edinburgh University Press, 1967.

—————. "Mohammedanism in West Africa," *Methodist Quarterly Review* 31:62 (1871).

—————. "The Negro in Ancient History," *Methodist Quarterly Review* 29:71 (1869).

DuBois, W.E. Burghardt. *The Negro.* New York: Oxford University Press, 1970. (Originally Published in 1915).

Elkins, Stanley M. *Slavery: A Problem in American Institutional and Intellectual Life.* Chicago: University of Chicago Press, 1968.

Fortes, Meyer. *Oedipus and Job in West African Religion.* Cambridge, England: Cambridge University Press, 1959.

Frazier, E. Franklin. *The Negro Church in America.* New York: Schocken, 1963.

Graham, Shirley. *There Was Once a Slave: The Heroic Story of Frederick Douglass.* New York: Messner, 1968.

Hayford, J. E. Casely. *Ethiopia Unbound: Studies in Race Emancipation.* Second Edition. London: Frank Cass and Company, Ltd., 1969.

Heartman, Charles F., ed. *Phyllis Wheatley: Poems and Letters.* New York: C. F. Heartman, 1915.

Hill, Adelaide C. and Martin Kilson, eds. *Apropos of Africa.* London: Frank Cass and Company, Ltd., 1969.

Jahn, Janheinz. *Muntu: The New African Culture* (translated by Marjorie Grene). New York: Grove Press, Inc., 1961.

James, Cyril R. *The Black Jacobins.* New York: Random House, 1963.

Lynch, Hollis. *Edward Wilmot Blyden: Pan-Negro Patriot 1832-1912.* New York: Oxford University Press, 1970.

Mays, Benjamin E. *The Negro's God.* Boston: Chapman and Grimes, Inc., 1938.

Meier, August. *Negro Thought in America 1800-1915.* Ann Arbor, Michigan: University of Michigan Press, 1963.

Redkey, Edwin S. *Black Exodus: Black Nationalist and Back to Africa Movements 1890-1910.* New Haven: Yale Univ. Press, 1969.

Shepperson, George and Thomas Price. *Independent African.* Edinburgh: Edinburgh University Press, 1958.

Smith, M. G., Roy Augier and Rex Nettleford. *The Rastafari Movement in Kingston, Jamaica.* University College of the West Indies: Institute of Social and Economic Research, 1960. Reprint 1968.

Sundkler, Bengt. *Bantu Prophets in South Africa.* Second Edition. New York: Oxford University Press, 1961.